Not Your Mother's Mystic

Awakening isn't about escaping life. It's about igniting it.

Kathryn Brewer

Golden Age Enterprises LLC

Dedication

To my children, Libby and Cameron—my heart, my why, my everything.

To my dad who always knew I'd be a writer and supported me in all my boldest ideas. To my mom who taught me how to care deeply and always be creative and to my brother who is always looking out for me.

To the family and friends who never wavered—especially Jae, who saw me when I couldn't see myself, and Kristin, who never doubts me.

And to my friends in spirit who have guided, ignited, and supported me—especially Bobby Maloney, Aleia Jade, Kelley and Kym.

Contents

Prologue

I was standing in my attic, staring at my dismantled Christmas tree—the one I'd carried upstairs in a tearful rage two days before Christmas to bury like a corpse, only to have to resurrect it just because my boyfriend Gunther finally texted me back. I was going to have to put Christmas back together like nothing ever happened.

For years, this had been my pattern: cycling between heartbreak and hope, between destroying things and desperately trying to fix them before the damage got out of control, before anyone noticed. I was drowning in debt, hiding my tears from my kids, and praying for relief while simultaneously wondering if it would be easier not to exist at all.

I never imagined that within months, I'd have full clarity on my life's purpose, access to divine direction on what move to make next, and complete confidence that the openness and passion that made me vulnerable in relationships, the very thing I was constantly trying to "fix" was the best thing about me. And I'd know, without any doubt or hesitation, something about myself that seemed, in that moment, impossible to believe—that there was nothing wrong with me, that everything would be okay, that I was loved and lovable.

Transformation doesn't always arrive when we're ready, or looking for it. Sometimes it finds us in our most broken moments, or while we're simply folding laundry on an ordinary Tuesday afternoon.

Chapter One

Losing Myself

I used to think heartbreak meant losing someone else until I lost myself. By the time I noticed the emptiness, the person who once had hopes and dreams was gone. There was a time when I wanted to be a playwright, crafting stories that moved people to tears or laughter. I studied English in college, wrote stories and poetry and imagined myself living an artistic life, filled with creativity and adventure.

Instead, I found myself crunching numbers in a cubicle, trying to keep up with an endless flow of deadlines. I was constantly stressed, had horrible anxiety and struggled to make time for friends or fun. My spare time was spent working in second and third jobs to make ends meet as a single mother of two. As stressful as my day job was, it still didn't pay the bills.

My romantic life followed the same downward spiral. Once a believer in love, I found myself divorced with a string of heartbreak and painful memories.

No matter how hard I worked, financial security remained just out of reach. Each month, I slipped deeper into debt despite my efforts. I'd check my bank account multiple times a day to make sure there was something left. When it got in the double digits, I'd find something in my house to sell on Facebook Marketplace to bridge the gap. I sold my kids old sporting supplies, old clothes, electronics. This life—this existence—wasn't what I had planned, but changing course seemed impossible.

Everyone else appeared to navigate their lives with maps I never received. If life came with instructions, mine were missing crucial pages.

Gunther and I met at the Oil Change place on Hwy 17. He had a Pittsburgh Steelers hat on and the accent to match. He sounded like home. My friend Molly's husband, Connor was there too. He knew us both.

"You're both from Pittsburgh! Have you met?" Connor asked, not knowing the path this introduction would take.

Gunther and I introduced ourselves. I reached out to shake his hand. He held it firmly, my own hand got swallowed up in the size of his. I was drawn to his light blue eyes. He looked at me like he was trying to figure me out.

"You going to watch the game today?" he asked.

"I'm not into sports," I said.

After that initial introduction, I started to see him everywhere. He was on the other side of the pump at the gas station, filling up his truck. He was pushing a grocery cart toward me from the other end of the aisle. He was sitting in the bleachers, our son's playing on the same lacrosse team. He was recently divorced. His ex-wife would sit in a different part of the bleachers. My ex-husband and his second wife would sit near the front. Gunther and I started to sit together.

I saw nothing but green lights. I was hopeful I'd never have to date again. I was tired of doing everything for myself.

The weekend before Memorial Day he stopped by my house to drop off some herbs he'd been growing in his garden before he went out of town with his kids.

"These are so good for you," he said. You can eat them raw if you want or chop them up and season with them." He pulled some leaves off the stems and tossed them in his mouth.

"So good," he said. He pulled off some more and fed them to me. His eyes twinkling to see how I'd react.

It tasted earthy and fresh. "So good." I replied.

Then he leaned down and kissed me. We were just inside the back door next to the laundry room. I took a step backwards and he pressed his body against mine against the laundry room door. His mouth was hot and fresh from the herbs. His hands ran up and down my sides.

"So good," he said again.

"So good," I repeated.

Things moved fast after that first kiss. It was easy. Our kids were already friends. He lived a mile away. Our routines were similar. School drop-off, sports, cooking. The weather was getting warmer, the days were longer. Life was blooming. I was so happy I'd catch myself singing and skipping. I couldn't stop myself. My fairytale had finally come true.

We went fishing together on the surf. Our fishing poles in front of our chairs. We'd talk and watch the tips for action. He seemed to catch fish after fish. I didn't catch anything, but I didn't care. I was just glad to be there with him.

Within months we were inseparable. It was just assumed we'd be spending time together after work or on weekends. Even our kids got along. All close in age, there was a lot of activity, even chaos but it was fun. They were all busy and had their own personalities. They came over to play Wii sports in my living room, so many kids they filled both couches. Gunther sat on the floor, playing right along with them. We went to his house to grill out. Before anyone took a bite we'd drop our heads, and Gunther would lead us in prayer.

He didn't drink. Neither did I. He loved God. So, did I.

All my hesitation fell away, and I let myself fall head over heels in love, deeper than I ever knew was possible. He did too.

We planned to spend Christmas together. It was going to feel like we had a big family between his three boys and my boy and girl. I couldn't have made it more perfect if I'd designed it all by hand.

Gunther had to travel a lot with work. I missed him when he was gone but it allowed me to focus on my responsibilities. It was easy to be consumed. It was a week before Christmas, and he was packing for a final three-day trip. I was sitting in his bed watching him pack. He'd told me recently that he was getting along better with his ex-wife. He attributed it to me and to our relationship that everything seemed to be going better, including his communication with her. I was glad to hear it but also wondering why he was telling me that.

Old insecurities resurfaced. Is he missing her? Is he hoping to rekindle things?

"I got your gift already," he said. I was both excited and nervous about this. I hadn't received a romantic gift for a holiday, birthday, anything, in years. My ex-husband thought gifts were a waste of money. "Only kids have birthdays and presents. If you need something, just buy it," he'd say. Then he'd comb through the bank statements questioning the necessity of anything I bought.

I'd already bought Gunther's gift too. I bought it in October.

"It was so weird," Gunther said. "I found something I know you'll really love. It just looks like something you would love. But when I was standing there at the register to buy it, I had this surreal experience. For the last twenty years I've bought something for Annie for Christmas. But this year, I'm buying something for you."

I felt the saliva pooling in my throat. Why is he buying a gift for me and thinking about his ex-wife? I was so tired of hearing her name!

My heart was pounding. Time slowed down. Then the words tumbled out of my mouth, harsh and uncaring.

"If you bought me something at the same store you bought something for her the past twenty years then I don't even want it. I can't just be a replacement. I'm my own person!"

He turned to look at me, still holding a half-folded tee shirt in his hands. His eyes went dark.

"Get out."

I froze.

"Get the fuck out of my house."

I couldn't move. I didn't understand what was happening. I couldn't remember what I'd said. I couldn't remember what had just happened. I knew I said something about not wanting the present, and his wife. I must have said something else also. The room felt cold.

He threw the shirt on the bed and walked over to me. Like I was under a spell, I stood up. I couldn't breathe. He followed me to the front door, opened it and threw me out. I wasn't even wearing my shoes.

Chapter Two

Talking to God

I cried for three days. I couldn't concentrate. I couldn't sleep. I called him. It went straight to voicemail. I texted. No reply. I drove past his house. His car was gone.

Would he be back for Christmas? Or was he going to spend the holiday with his adult daughter out of state? For every question, my mind made up answers. None of them good.

My kids were with their dad. The house was quiet, my thoughts anything but. I kept refreshing my phone, scrolling back through our texts, humiliated by the sheer number of messages I'd sent. Paragraphs.

I called friends, hoping someone could explain what I couldn't. They said what I said was hurtful. They also said his reaction was extreme.

But none of that helped. I couldn't take it back.

I called my cousin Jae. She didn't take a side. She didn't read into it. She just said, "All I know is God takes knee-mail. Take your worries to God. That's going to be your best bet."

Jae and I had been each other's lifelines for years, connected by blood but bonded through shared disappointments. While I was dealing with financial struggles and relationship disasters, she was navigating her own heavy burdens. She had lost both her parents. Her mother passed on Jae's own birthday, a cruel twist of fate that left a permanent mark on what should have been a day of celebration.

She lived in New York and I was living in North Carolina, but despite the physical distance between us, we maintained a connection that sustained us both. Our friendship survived through late-night phone calls, lengthy text exchanges, and the rare visit.

In many ways, we were mirrors for each other, both dealing with men who couldn't or wouldn't meet our needs. Her husband slept in a separate room, emotionally disconnected, while she put her own dreams on indefinite hold to raise their children and support his career.

We recognized in each other the familiar pattern of giving too much and receiving too little. She never pushed her advice on me or judged my choices, even when they were obviously self-destructive. Instead, she offered unwavering support. When everyone else was telling me what to do about Gunther, she simply reminded me she would be there for me, no matter what.

In those days after being thrown out of Gunther's house, I listened to her guidance. Every time the grief crept in, I hit the floor. I prayed.

Sometimes in reverence, showing great faith and trust in His will. Then within minutes, I was yelling at God, pleading with Him to fix it.

My bowels were a wreck. Everything I ate went right through me. My head hurt.

I had to distract myself, so I rearranged my bedroom. Then when that was done, I went into the living room and saw my tree staring back at me with all its glittery ornaments and twinkly lights.

"Fuck Christmas anyway," I thought. It had been five days since the incident. It was two days until Christmas. I hadn't heard from Gunther. I guess I was going to spend it alone after all. Once again.

I decided to take down my tree. Christmas was officially over. I removed all the stupid cheap shiny plastic balls and then the dumb K-Mart ornaments and threw them away. No use saving them. Christmas was dead to me. I took the strings of lights off and threw them back in the Tupperware crate I stored them in. I imagined myself lifting the entire tree and launching it into the sky like a javelin, having it land right on Gunther's house, piercing his roof.

It was a fake tree. It cost almost four hundred dollars. As much as I wanted to get rid of it, even in my tantrum, I was financially practical. I disassembled it, piece by piece, and carried it to the attic like a burial.

All signs of Christmas were deleted from my house. I didn't feel good, but I did feel better, temporarily.

I kept going back to my phone to see if there was a message from Gunther.

The grief over losing the relationship hit me in waves. When it hit again, again I hit the ground on my knees, praying to God.

This time, I pleaded with God to help me understand. If he's not for me, I will accept that but why the silence? Why won't he even talk to me God? I'm trying so hard to reach out to him and he doesn't even reply. He's not even listening! Why God! Why won't he talk to me!?

God spoke to me in my grief. I felt his words inside my head, "Why don't you talk to me?" He asked back, convicting me. I knew exactly what He meant in those words.

What holds me back from talking to God in all those times I "forget about Him?" When I'm not suffering, when I'm not asking for something. When life is good? Why do I only show up at God's feet to plead and pray when I want something from Him?

Gunther's reasons for not talking to me were the same as my reason for not talking to God: selfishness, stubbornness, thinking I knew what was best, entitlement, lack of integrity.

I was both humbled by His answer and in awe that I actually got an answer. Surely God had more important things to worry about than me and my midlife heartbreak.

"Thank you," I prayed, humbled. I vowed to turn to God instead of turning to Gunther. All I needed was God. I'd been told that a million times. I just needed live it.

Chapter Three

Relief

I finally slept. When I heard God's voice, the delirium finally broke like a fever, and I started to breathe again. I took a shower, got back into bed and slept. I finally woke up in a daze and made coffee without even looking at my phone. I had been acting like a maniac after being hurtful. I didn't deserve forgiveness. I needed to work on myself. I was in the wrong and that was too bad for me, but no one owed me anything.

I thought of God all morning and how His words were so brief but held so much clarity. And while I felt corrected, I didn't feel punished or judged. I was helped. I was comforted. I was guided.

I fed the chickens and the dog. I texted my kids to tell them how much I loved them. I prayed for my kids and my parents and my cousin and everyone I could think of that they could feel the peace I was feeling in that moment. I even prayed for Gunther to have peace in his heart.

When I finally looked at my phone, there was a text on the notification screen. It was from Gunther. I sat on the floor and opened the message.

"Hey."

That's all he said. Just "hey."

"Hey," I texted back.

"What are you doing?" he replied.

"Just sitting here," I texted back.

"Lol."

"I'm sorry," I texted.

"I'm sorry too," he replied. My eyes filled with tears.

"Are you home?" I asked

"I get home tonight," he texted.

Then I dared to ask, "Are you still coming over for Christmas tomorrow?"

"Yes. That's what we planned."

The relief flooded over me. Everything seemed normal, like nothing had ever happened. Had I overreacted? I'd spent almost a week crying, completely incapacitated. But for him, he was still planning to follow through on our plans.

Then I remembered... the tree!

I ran up to the attic in my pajamas and hauled the tree back downstairs.

"Why am I like this?" I admonished myself. Once the tree was standing, I threw on my clothes and drove into town. What was even going to be open on Christmas eve!?

Hobby Lobby was open. I pushed my cart to the decorations section, passing other shoppers like I was driving in the fast lane.

I didn't even know how many ornaments to buy. I tried to visualize the same amount I'd thrown away. I only needed to fill the front. The back of a tree was in the corner. I chose some pretty white and gold ornaments. They came in boxes of six. The gold ones glittered; the white ones were pearly. I bought some thick wired gold ribbon to cut and tie bows on the branches. I checked out less than fifteen minutes before the store closed.

When I got home, I put on Christmas music and decorated my tree, for the second time.

The next morning, I made sausage links, hash browns, pancakes and cinnamon rolls. Gunther and his boys filled the house with noise and laughter. I had presents for his kids that they opened and compared with each other, thanking me warmly.

I gave Gunther his gift.

"I don't have a gift for you," he said. "I returned it last week. You said you didn't want it."

"I know," I said. "I understand."

"Those aren't the same ornaments you had last time we were here," his son announced. His brothers dismissed him. "I swear!" he exclaimed! They were red and gold before. These are totally different! I swear!" He turned to me, "Did you change them?"

"Of course she didn't change them," his brother interjected. "That's totally crazy. We were just here last week. People don't just change their ornaments."

"They look nice," Gunther chimed in. "They look the same to me."

I wondered if he noticed and was protecting me by letting it slide, or was it all the same to him? Life just moving forward like any old day, while I felt like I'd been trapped in a tornado and just got spit back out.

Chapter Four

The Grind

L ife slipped back into place. The holidays passed, and we moved into spring like nothing had happened. We didn't talk much about our fight. We just agreed we were both wrong and both sorry. That was enough.

We had pizza nights with Wii sports and board games. The kids made a family play list on Spotify. None of them knew that this bliss had nearly shattered irreparably. It all happened in the background, while they were with their other parents. I was so grateful to have been given this second chance, but it did feel different. I was afraid of messing up again. Everything was tenuous.

Gunther was still traveling with work, but we talked on the phone while he was driving or from his hotel. Then the world suddenly shut down. Covid hit. The world was afraid, me especially.

Gunther was trying to get his work complete, but I kept calling and telling him that schools would be cancelled.

"It's going to happen," I said.

"How do you know?" he challenged.

"I just know. And it's on the news."

"It's under control," he assured me.

"I hope it is, but I don't think it is," I was doubtful.

I was buying extra food at the store. I was afraid for my kids. The news announced a case in Washington. Then another case. I was glued to twitter, day and night.

I told my ex-husband to get extra food. I told my parents to get extra food. I told my friends to get extra food. I told Gunther to get extra food. He wasn't as concerned as I was, so I got enough food for him and his boys if it came to that.

"Did you see there is a case without a source?" I mentioned on the phone.

"What's that even mean?" he asked.

"It means it's not contained. It's going to spread."

"I can't deal with you. All this Chicken Little shit." he said. "Leave me alone."

He hung up. It had happened again.

Chapter Five

Shutting Down

Then everything shut down. My already stressful job became exponentially harder. The pressure was mounting. Supply chains were breaking, nerves were fraying. People started hoarding toilet paper. Schools closed and suddenly we became teachers to our kids on top of everything else.

Who was I to prioritize sleep, rest, personal time, eating when there were people dying?

My standard issue anxiety went into full blown panic, and I existed in this highly alert, very frightened, over exerted state for weeks.

I cancelled plans, became obsessed with hand washing and worried over every cough or throat clearing. I even cancelled my son's birthday. Worse, instead of spending the day with him, I worked late and went to bed in tears.

My son, thoughtful and sensitive, hid his disappointment. Instead of thinking of himself, he worried over me. He wanted to help. He wanted me to take a break. Watching me struggle has given him an inner drive to work hard to avoid the kind of stress he's grown up with. He doesn't ever want to feel the fear of a missed bill, the disappointment of not being able to participate because of money or the anguish of survival mode. In short, he wants a life very different from the one I've given him. I didn't want my kids to live like this, anymore. I didn't want to live like this either.

Chapter Six

Therapy

My therapist, Joe was a kind, older man with an office decorated like a library. We met on Zoom because everything was shut down from Covid. He had a light brown beard and a perpetually askew collar that resisted his otherwise orderly demeanor. He sat in a wingback chair, flanked by tall bookshelves filled with serious-looking books. No matter what I said, Joe greeted me with a warm smile and compassionate eyes.

Joe wanted to know why I was in therapy. "What's brought you here?" he asked, like I'd just wandered into his little shop of wholesome advice while passing by.

It was embarrassing. I was a college-educated mother of two with a good job who loved to write and had friends who loved her, but I couldn't get over a breakup. And now I was hoping this stranger could fix me.

Joe listened thoughtfully as I admitted, "I think I'm controlling. My expectations are unreasonable, and I get upset when things don't go my way."

"Are you controlling?"

"I don't know. I guess..."

"Give me an example of controlling."

"Sometimes we make plans," I offered, "and when he changes his mind, I can't let it go. It's like I can't shake it. Last week we were going to get breakfast. We get breakfast together often on Sundays, and I was looking forward to it, but he never came by to pick me up. I texted to see if he was running late, but he didn't respond. Then I told him I felt hurt because he should have told me if the plans were changing, but he says he doesn't have to tell me everything. And then I get really upset."

"Describe 'really upset.'"

"I cry. I tell him he's being hurtful. I tell him he should have communicated if the plans were changing because I was looking forward to it."

"What does he say to that?"

"He says I have too many expectations."

"Do you?"

"Yes, it sounds like I do."

"And what else is going on?"

"I just can't stop thinking about him. I get so jealous that he's talking to other women. It's obsessive. I think about him all the time. He says I'm stalking him."

"Are you?"

"Kind of."

"Tell me about this."

"I noticed he was adding all these half-dressed girls on Instagram. I told him it hurt my feelings to see him commenting on their pictures, but he never commented on mine. He said I was insecure, and it was just Instagram."

This was so hard to say. I felt like I was really exposing myself but if I couldn't be honest in therapy, then why even go?

"Then, he blocked me. He said it wouldn't bother me anymore if I couldn't see his account. So, I created a fake account, and I would log into my fake account and see he was still adding those girls. It's like I go looking for things to hurt my own feelings. Then, I bring it up to him. I try not to but then it just comes out and it upsets him. He wants me to drop it, but I can't. I said if he was with me, he shouldn't be messaging them."

"How do you know he was messaging them? Did you go into his phone?"

"I asked him. I asked if he was talking to them. He said he only messaged them to share the gospel."

"Do you believe that?"

I could feel myself shrinking. My shoulders curled inward. My breath went shallow. I was trying to disappear. I was aware how insane I sounded. I'd always just felt all my feelings. Saying them out loud made them sound different. I'd have to be a moron to believe a fifty-year-old man was messaging half-naked twenty-something girls on social media because he wanted to save them by sharing the gospel.

I was a moron.

I believed him. At least I tried to. I didn't have a choice not to. If I didn't believe him, I'd have to consider that he was blatantly lying to me, that he was intentionally disrespecting me, that he was hurtful on purpose. And that would mean the relationship was over. Worse, that it was never real to begin with, and I'd lost two more years of my life catering to a man who didn't care about me.

Which would mean I hadn't loved and lost, I'd just lost and lost.

"He's got really strong faith in God," I said. "He goes to church every Sunday and stands right in the front with his hands held all the way up to the heavens and sings his heart out. He prays constantly. He'll even put his hands on strangers to pray for them."

"So, you believe him," Joe wanted me to clarify.

"I want to," I said.

Chapter Seven

Going Back

S ocial activities were still limited from the pandemic. The kids were learning remotely, I was working remotely. Church was telecast. We could go weeks without seeing anyone in person besides each other. Before we broke up the third time (or was it the fourth?), Gunther had built a chicken coop for me in my back yard. Before it was completed, I'd done something to upset him and then I had to finish it myself.

Becoming more self-sufficient seemed as good a distraction as any. I got a circular saw from Home Depot. I learned how to cut straight lines and angles. With each hardware screw I drove into the wood, I developed a stronger sense of autonomy. I painted the coop inside and outside, surrounded it with hardware cloth to keep out the predators, screwed hinges on the doors. But when it came to finishing the roof, I knew I would need help, expert help.

My kids were at their dad's house for the week and a storm was coming. I needed Gunther. It had been months since I'd spoken with him. I wasn't sure if Gunther was the only one who could help me or if I was finding an excuse to reach out to him. But after months of therapy with Joe, I wanted to believe I was stronger, smarter and healed enough to move into something better with Gunther. Something like friendship.

Maybe there was a way of staying connected without the attachment. Like adults.

"Hi Gunther," I texted in my professional, mature, healed tone. "I hope you are doing well. I need some help with this roof and was wondering if you might be available to help any time in the next week."

Within fifteen minutes, he was at my house with his tools. Ten minutes after that, we were in my bed.

We spent the rest of the day together. He told me about all the chickens he had hatched. He'd leased ten acres of pasture to start a poultry farm. He was so excited telling me, and I was hanging on every word.

"I got an industrial size incubator." His eyes were twinkling. "I've been hatching hundreds of chicks."

"Baby chickens? You have hundreds of baby chickens?" I had to see them. I had to know everything about them. I was jealous of those chickens getting to spend all that time with him, getting all his attention. How could I resist baby chickens?

The metal pieces for the roof were already at my house, and the frame was solid, but I needed help getting them lifted up and placed. And I didn't know how to fasten them.

He brought his big ladder with him and together we got the metal roofing layed out over the frame. He talked me through it from below, telling me exactly how much overlap I needed.

"Now drill in the holes! You've got to really lean into it!" he shouted, encouraging me.

I leaned my whole body into in and the screw pushed down with a final squeal as it tightened on the roof. It was secure in the wood behind it.

When the roof was done, I roared with pride and satisfaction.

"I did it!" I shouted. I held my arms up and shook my fists in victory.

Gunther took a picture of me. I looked strong, happy and capable.

After that, we grabbed something to eat. Then he asked if I wanted to go look at all his baby chickens. You know I wanted to! And just like that, we were back together. Back to our old banter, back in love as if the past four months of separation and pain never happened.

"You can sell those baby chicks and get some money coming in to cover feed costs," I said. "I can build you a website."

"I don't know about that," he said. "I'm so busy."

"I can help."

The next week, I created a Shopify website and developed a logo with someone on Fiverr. Then, I finished the website, made a list of shipping supplies to buy, and ordered business cards.

When the business cards arrived with his name on them, I gave them to him. He loved them.

And with that our romance took on a new level. We were friends, lovers, and business partners. He built the coops, I handled marketing. I couldn't have imagined a better life. I was in heaven.

Then, Gunther fired me and dumped me. He accused me of being too controlling.

"It's my business, not yours," he said.

The ground fell out from under me. This was supposed to be our dream, our shared passion, but suddenly it was just his. Once again, I wanted to believe the fantasy, but the truth crashed down. I'd ignored the warnings, free-falling into heartbreak, blindsided by the reality I'd refused to see.

I couldn't do it anymore. The cycle was draining me. I was hiding from my kids in my room so I could cry for hours. I had to stop. It was time to try something different.

Chapter Eight

Breakthroughs with Natalie

I went back to therapy, this time with a new therapist named Natalie. Just like with Joe, I was hoping she could fix me. Unlike Joe, she didn't ask why I acted the way I did. She didn't dwell on why or ask the history of the relationship. She wanted to know my goals. She wanted me to envision a future where I was happy. She told me about neuroplasticity and gave me homework.

"Where do you want to see yourself in three months and a year?"

The pandemic was lifting. There were more opportunities to go out and do things. I made an effort to see her in person. The forty-five minute drive to her office felt important, a break from the isolation of working from home. I balanced Zoom appointments with in-person visits, sometimes taking the day off to run errands and clear my head.

Leaving the house felt liberating. The convenience of working at home plus the pandemic meant that I would sometimes go weeks without leaving my house for more than groceries.

Her office, nestled in a growing arts district, reminded me of Portland in the late nineties. The building had a co-working space with exposed brick walls and a small coffee bar. Natalie's office was simple yet eclectic, with quirky lamps that added to its charm.

"It's a classic dilemma," she said, reviewing my homework. "You have conflicting values. Your loyalty and compassion are compromising your self-respect."

No judgment, just a fact. Before I could even feel defensive, she moved on.

"One thing I've noticed during our sessions is that you're deeply committed. When you invest yourself, you go all in."

"Is that bad?" I asked.

"Of course not!" she replied. "It's great!"

"Then why am I miserable? Why am I stuck in these cycles?"

"First of all, it really doesn't matter why. The important thing is to recognize that this is a core trait. It's who you are. You can't change who you are."

"True," I agreed, "I've tried, and it never works."

"But what you can do is adjust how you express these traits, and where you direct them."

"I'm not following," I felt anxious. What was she saying?

"Acknowledge who you are and redirect that energy toward people and things that value you."

"Who? Where?" I was frustrated. I'd tried to move on. I went on dates, even had a fling, but always ran back to Gunther. It felt impossible.

"You."

"Me?"

"Yes," she said, leaning forward with her elbows on her knees. "What if," she tried again, "you took all these great characteristics of yours," she picked up my values and traits homework pages, "and used them on yourself?"

I felt like I'd heard this before. "Love yourself." But how? I didn't need platitudes, I needed help. I needed action. I needed a to-do list.

"Everything you did for Gunther—the way you always saw the best in him, the way you forgave him for everything big and small, the way you believed in him—those are your traits. Those traits belong to you. You can choose where you direct them. What if all that faith and grace and patience you give to others, you give in yourself instead?

"What if," she continued as I tried to take it all in. "What if the best thing you can give to the people you love is the best version of yourself?"

It had never occurred to me that my constant sacrifice wasn't what other people wanted from me. What they really wanted was for me to be happy and whole. For them, I was willing to try.

Chapter Nine

Investing in Myself

W hat did I love before I loved Gunther? I hadn't asked myself that question in so long, and the answer didn't come easily at first. But as I sat with it, the memories came back. I made a list.

I loved to write. I loved to be in nature. I loved spending time with my kids and with friends. I loved live music. I loved live performance of any kind, especially theater. I loved to read.

Then, I tasked myself with finding ways to re-engage with these things.

I joined a writing workshop and resumed work on the novel I'd started in 2017, before I met Gunther. The workshop, which met online weekly, became a space where I could share my work and offer feedback to others. Connecting via Zoom felt almost as natural as meeting in person, and it reminded me that living in a small, remote location didn't limit my access to creative communities like it used to. There were writers from all over the US and Canada in the workshop.

I also found ways to be more active and explore the local area. When my kids were with their dad, I'd drive north to New Bern, rent a kayak, and paddle for hours, feeling the wind on my skin, watching the sunlight rippling on the water.

The sounds of birds diving and fish jumping brought me back to myself, reminding me of the beauty I'd seen in places like Mount Hood in Oregon, and Wind River Wilderness, the Boundary Waters of Minnesota and Canada. I hadn't been able to travel since my divorce but that didn't mean I wouldn't do it again. Even just an hour up the road was an opportunity to see something different. I could explore all kinds of places within a couple hours' drive and be back at home to sleep by dark. It reminded me of how big, promising, and full of opportunity the world was outside the four walls of my house where I'd been hiding. In those quiet moments, I started to believe I could reclaim that beauty in my own life.

Meanwhile, I continued therapy with Natalie. I found myself thinking less about Gunther and more about the life I could build on my own. Even though I still thought about him and had the urge to contact him, I didn't act on it. I was sleeping better, crying less, and things were genuinely improving. I felt good.

One evening, while helping my daughter with her college applications, I kept getting redirected to the graduate school page for University of North Carolina in Wilmington. At first, I was frustrated. She was applying for undergrad, and not even at UNCW. She wanted to go to NC State. But after it happened again, I decided to read the page.

Graduate classes were starting on a rolling basis. "Apply Now and start classes in a couple weeks!" The banner kept popping up, impossible to close.

I'd considered going to grad school years ago, it felt like lifetimes ago. I was accepted into the Information Sciences program at University of Washington in Seattle. I never enrolled. Instead, I moved to California and married my ex-husband. I remembered how good it felt to be accepted into grad school with the promise of specializing in something, getting deep into the details. But I was too old now, too broke and didn't even know what I would do with a graduate degree. I scolded myself for even lingering. I was supposed to be helping my daughter, not getting lost in daydreams for myself.

I navigated away from the page and found the information my daughter needed, but the thought of applying lingered. Would I ever go back to school? Could it help me gain the skills to get a better job? I looked up the costs for the test and study materials, and it was far too expensive. The books alone were several hundred dollars and then there was the fee to take the test. What a ridiculous idea. I put the thought, and the possibility, aside. Then I remembered, entrance exams had been waived for undergraduates due to COVID and still hadn't been reinstated. My daughter wasn't required to submit hers she applied to college.

Many kids never even took the test. What if they were waived for grad school too? I brought up a browser on my phone, gazing at the too bright glow of the screen and confirmed it. There was no GRE requirement. All I needed were two references, an application, and a $75 fee.

"If I apply to grad school, will you write a reference letter for me?" I texted my cousin Jae. It was 11pm.

"You're applying to grad school?"

"Let's not get sidetracked. Will you?"

"Of course."

I filled out the application on my phone. This was crazy! I didn't have $75 to spare, and I definitely couldn't afford grad school! But for once, I wanted a good feeling just for me. I hesitated, my thumb hovering over the "submit" button. Was it reckless? Maybe. But in that moment, I craved the feeling of possibility more than I feared the risk. So, I hit submit.

The next week, the admissions counselor called me. I was in. The acceptance letter was in my inbox. I was accepted. I was chosen. I had value. If I wanted to attend, I could start as soon as three weeks. But of course, I wasn't going to do that.

Chapter Ten

Embracing Change

"I did something crazy," I told Natalie.

"I'll be the judge of crazy," she joked.

"Right." I laughed. "That's your job."

"What did you do?"

"Well, it felt reckless and irresponsible, but also good. Nothing will come of it, though. It was just a good ego boost!"

"What was it?" she asked with excitement, enjoying my enthusiasm.

"I filled out an application to grad school."

"And?"

"I got in!"

"Congratulations!" she exclaimed. "I had no idea you were looking into grad school."

"I didn't either," I confessed. "I applied on a whim."

"This is wonderful news! What will your degree be?"

"It's an online degree program for an MBA, but I'm not going to actually go," I replied, thinking it should have been obvious.

"Why not?"

The most obvious reason was money. But underneath that was the heavier truth: I didn't believe I would do well. I had always struggled under pressure, and the thought of facing exams, deadlines, and the possibility of failure sent my stomach into knots. It was safer not to try.

"I can't afford it," I said, hoping that would put the idea to rest.

"If you could afford to go, would you go?"

The thought of having the money to attend school was so wildly impossible that it felt safe to say yes, even though money wouldn't erase my insecurities about my academic abilities.

"I guess. Yeah, probably."

"Your employer will probably pay for it," she said. "See if you can find out."

I hadn't considered that. Natalie had simultaneously called my bluff and ignited a flicker of hope. What if it was possible? Would it make a difference in my career? Would it make a difference in my finances? Would it make a difference in my life?

I told myself once I got my kids launched successfully into adulthood, I'd figure it out. I'd sell my house, live in my car, move in with my parents. I'd scale back to almost nothing so I could put everything into paying off my debt. I joked with my kids about living in a tent in their back yards when they have their own homes. "It will be just me and a couple chickens. You'll barely notice us!" It would have been funnier if I wasn't serious. But maybe there was another path. Maybe I should try?

Chapter Eleven

Progress

Almost six months had passed since I started seeing Natalie, and so much had changed. I was no longer consumed by the same questions that had once kept me up at night. Instead of wondering why Gunther behaved the way he did, I was finally focused on something far more important: how to direct my energy toward building a life that was good for me and my kids. It didn't have to be permanent. It was an experiment. Yet, it was helping. I hadn't talked to Gunther, hadn't reached out, and hadn't run into him. He hadn't reached out to me either. I'd gone at least a few months without crying.

Every spare moment that could have been spent socializing or even just relaxing was now devoted to homework. The MBA wasn't just a goal; it was a lifeline, something tangible I could work toward. Enrolling felt like proof that I wasn't stuck anymore. I wasn't sure if I was healing or just too busy to feel sorry for myself, but either way, it felt like progress.

"I'm not where I want to be, but I'm on the right path," I reminded myself whenever that critical voice in my head pointed out that I wasn't as far along as I'd hoped.

I had redirected my energy, like Natalie recommended, and as a result the trajectory of my life was pointing in a new direction. The destination was far in the distance, but at least it was in my sights.

My sessions with Natalie were starting to feel like check-ins with a friend. I was busy. Nothing dramatic or exciting was going on because I didn't have time for it. We talked more about how I could support and encourage my kids than we talked about me.

I had a break in classes coming up for winter holidays.

"What are you planning to do with your time off?" Natalie asked during one of our sessions.

I started rattling off my to-do list: "First, start working on my taxes so I can get any refund ASAP, organize my attic, gather things for a garage sale, pressure wash the house, clean out the chicken coops, lose weight, exercise, win the lottery."

"Some of that can wait," she interrupted.

I wondered which part. They all felt overdue and urgent.

"Why don't you go have some fun?"

"Fun?" I tensed up.

"Come on. I know you have friends. You always say you don't have time for them. Give them a call. What do you like to do?"

I drew a blank.

"You can do this," she challenged.

"The things I like to do are too expensive and too far away."

"Such as?"

"I love theater, live music, gallery openings. I love cities. I love to travel. I love to be debt free. I love having clean chicken coops."

"This town has a vibrant theater scene. It's not Broadway, but it's not bad either."

I hadn't investigated any cultural events in a long time. It was a 40-minute drive into town at best. I didn't think my friends liked shows and theater. Everyone seemed to just go to bars and drink. I'd stopped drinking in 2018, and it had contributed to my sense of isolation, yet I felt physically better and slept better without alcohol.

"I'm sure you can think of something. Just get out of the house. Go somewhere. Maybe you'll meet someone."

"Like, a man?" The thought of opening up to anyone sent a wave of panic through me.

"Yes, like a man."

"I thought we were done investing in men and just investing in me," I replied.

"It's not mutually exclusive. You can invest in yourself and also share yourself with someone else."

That felt too risky. "I'm just getting the hang of this. I'm not ready to fall apart yet."

"Oh, don't be so negative. Look at all the things you have going for you right now! You've made great progress. You haven't talked to Gunther in months. You're far more capable than you give yourself credit for. Just keep an open mind."

I didn't say anything, but her words hung in the air. Maybe she was right. Maybe I was capable of more than I realized. But it still felt safer to stay where I was, in the controlled environment I'd built for myself.

Chapter Twelve

Dating Apps

My finger hovered over the "download" button. Was I really doing this again? I thought of Natalie's voice: "You don't need to change yourself to receive love."

It sounded like such a nice sentiment. But sentiments felt empty and dangerous to me now. It wasn't the dating that terrified me—it was the investing. The slow, deliberate way I'd hand over pieces of myself only to have them returned damaged or not at all.

I was cynical. I didn't want to be cynical. I also didn't want to get hurt. Between the kids, the chickens, and trying to rebuild what was left of my life, did I even have time to give someone else? And yet, the evenings stretched long and quiet.

I downloaded a dating app "out of curiosity" and created a profile "just to browse." I scrolled through my phone to see if I had any cute photos. Most of what I found were pictures of my kids, chickens, and motivational quotes. I hardly had any photos of just me.

I paused when I reached a picture of me with Gunther on the tractor at the farm.

It was the day he had a brand-new orange Kubota tractor delivered. I looked so happy, and frankly, so did he. I sat on his lap as he drove across the field, tilling up row after row of land. I had pulled my phone out of my pocket, extended my arm toward the trees in the distance, and snapped a picture of us together, cheek to cheek, smiling. Fresh-tilled dirt, stretching out in rows behind us into the horizon. I remembered the scent of grass, his sweat, earth turning beneath the wheels. "This can be fields of lavender for you," he had said to me, "And we can get bees. You've always wanted bees."

Everything was falling into place perfectly. Our future, rolling out in front of us as neatly as the rows being tilled behind us.

Three days later, he broke up with me. "You're so difficult," he'd said. "You think you know everything. I can't even be around you."

My throat tightened as I stared at the photo. Us on the tractor, Gunther smiling like everything we wanted was just one harvest away. My thumb hovered over the delete button, hesitating. The sting in my chest felt like someone was twisting something deep inside me. I pressed down. Whoosh. Gone.

I selected every photo of him I could find and hit delete again. Whoosh. I did it again. Whoosh. It felt reckless and dangerous. There was no going back.

As the photos reshuffled and disappeared from the screen, I wondered if true partnership was still possible. I wanted someone to create memories with, someone to reassure me when I was losing faith, someone to hold me when my anxiety got me spinning, someone who wouldn't need me to be smaller to make room for them. I missed having someone witness and share my life.

Maybe Natalie was right. Maybe I was ready to move on. Maybe it would be good for me to meet someone, even just for the opportunity to get out of the house and do something fun.

I found a couple of flattering photos of myself and uploaded them. The only full-body picture I could find was one of me standing in the hallway laughing, wearing jeans, a flannel shirt, and a red beanie, with one arm outstretched like I was ready to fight, and the other holding one of my hens. My daughter had taken the photo, teasing me about carrying a chicken through the house.

Here I was, back at the beginning.

I updated the profile requirements, making the distance short because I don't like driving and the age range narrow because I didn't want to match with Gunther if he was also online. I answered the questions honestly but briefly, making it as difficult as possible for anything to come from this, partly just to validate my own expectation of defeat.

I started swiping. It was early January. One of the prompts was to share a New Year's Resolution. Most of the men tried to make jokes. Some were sincere. My resolution was to keep investing in myself.

Most of the men posted selfies taken in their bathroom mirrors, their faces shadowed in dim fluorescent light with flecks of toothpaste splattered on the mirror like a depressing starry sky. They looked like they'd just witnessed something tragic, maybe it was their reflection. It was all the usual suspects: The strays: shirtless, unshaven, sad men who made me say, "For only twenty-five cents a day, you too can adopt a man." The throuples: married couples looking for a third. Then, of course, the Fake Hall Passes: men who would confess, "My wife won't have sex with me, so she told me to get on here." I'd think, "If the person legally bound to you won't have sex with you, why would anyone else?" No, thanks. And finally, the Regulars: all the faces I'd seen time and time again over the fifteen years I'd been single.

Seeing their faces served to remind me I was no different. I was a regular, too. Dating apps felt like the penal system of single adulthood. Once you're in the system, there's no getting out. You stay there, circling the drain for years.

But maybe somewhere in this digital purgatory was someone else who understood what it meant to try again after you promised yourself you wouldn't. Maybe someone else who would give me space to learn from my mistakes instead of punishing me for them. Someone who could be the positive, supporting encourager I needed so I wasn't having to do so much on my own.

Chapter Thirteen

James

I was about to close the app when I came across a profile that looked different from the others. He had a variety of photos in interesting locations participating in eclectic activities. He'd taken the time to complete every section of his profile. He must be new at this, I thought. Then I saw the reason why: he was a widower.

Friends had always said I should find a widower who enjoyed being married because he would want to marry again. He wouldn't have all the baggage of anger and resentment that came with divorce. The thought made me pause. Was I carrying that baggage myself now?

"Why not," I thought, and felt a small flutter of something that resembled hope.

I swiped and we instantly matched.

I asked about one of his pictures. He replied right away. He was light-hearted, chatty, and showed interest in me. He asked me questions and was responsive to my answers. Not the usual one-word responses that left me scrambling to keep conversation alive, wondering if I was boring or if they were just bad at communication. He was able to keep the conversation going and to let it go when we both had to attend to something else. It felt good and natural to interact with him, the digital equivalent of an easy breath after holding it for too long.

We texted back and forth for a couple of days and then I offered him my number. I wanted to hear his voice. I could tell a lot more by hearing his voice than I could with only texting. There were times I'd talked to someone on the phone, and they sounded decades older, or they were too distracted to follow a conversation. One time a man started telling a story and didn't stop for an hour. There was no way for me to cut him off, so I hung up on him.

James had a nice, engaging voice. When James spoke, there was no rush or distraction, no hint of nervousness or desperation to prove himself. His words were steady, confident. I didn't realize how much I needed that, someone who could make me feel seen, even just through the way he spoke. We had a lot in common: children the same age, roots in the cold northeast, a love of comedy and philosophy. We both worked nine-to-five.

After we hung up, I found myself smiling at nothing in particular as I filled the chickens' water. For once, I wasn't mentally rehearsing all the ways this could go wrong. I was simply present, feeling the weight of the water jug, hearing the birds cluck appreciatively, watching the sun set over my small piece of land that suddenly felt like it had room for someone else.

I told Natalie and my cousin about the date. Natalie was optimistic. My cousin just hoped he was normal. Jae had suffered through several of my dating attempts. It shocked her as much as it shocked me the many ways men were capable of behaving badly.

"Have you met him in person yet?" Natalie asked, her voice carrying that careful mix of excitement and caution that friends curate when you're dating again.

"Once," I said. "We met at a coffee shop and talked casually. It seemed to go well. We are still talking."

I had neutral leaning toward curious feelings about James. He was smart and successful. He had a dry sense of humor and loved to work out.

If I were being honest, he was very similar to men I'd met before. A marine (or ex-marine) with a punchy sense of humor. Loves jeeps, loves to work out, loves drinking. I'd been down this road before, the initial spark, the common interests, the gradual realization that we were fundamentally different in ways that mattered.

The one thing that was different about him so far was that he also loved to read books and could talk about them with enthusiasm and depth. It was a small thing, perhaps, but it felt significant. He gave me a hug at my car. He was tall so my face had to turn to the side and press against his chest to get close. When was my last hug? I wasn't sure about James, but I was sure I wanted more hugs.

"I guess we will see," I said, confessing that I was at least going to keep talking to him and there was a possibility for something more. The words felt both like surrender and a small act of courage.

"Yes," Natalie agreed with a glimmer in her eye. "We will see."

Chapter Fourteen

The Drive to the Game

"I have tickets to a hockey game," James said, his voice carrying a hint of anticipation. "Would you like to join me? It's this Saturday night. I'll pick you up at five. The drive to the game is about two hours, so we can grab a quick dinner near the arena. I'll have you home by midnight, one at the latest, if there's overtime."

True to his word, James arrived exactly at five. His casual style was effortlessly put together, his fitted pants and shirt highlighting a physique honed by regular workouts. He opened the car door for me, a small, thoughtful gesture that I didn't expect, which made me nearly collide with him trying to climb in the car.

Before pulling away, he asked, "Would you like the seat heater on?" His tone was genuinely considerate. I wondered if he was trying to impress me, or if this was simply who he was.

Our conversation flowed naturally, just as it had in text and on the phone. In the long drive, we covered favorite books, movies, childhood memories, and the small joys of life in our quiet town. He seemed to find more to appreciate about the town than I did, but then again, he enjoyed the water, boating, and he had disposable income I didn't have.

There was one topic we both avoided: his late wife. Her absence lingered between us, unspoken yet palpable. I wrestled with whether to bring it up, not wanting to overstep but also not wanting to seem indifferent.

"I'm sorry about your loss," I finally said, carefully choosing my words. "I want you to know that if you ever want to talk about her, I'm here to listen. And if you don't, that's okay too. I just didn't want you to think I was ignoring it or being uncaring."

James nodded, a subtle but meaningful gesture. "I appreciate that," he replied.

"What was her name?" I asked.

"Julie."

The car fell into a comfortable silence after that, the kind that doesn't necessarily need to be filled. I was glad I cleared the air. I turned my gaze to the window, watching as the world sped by, the steady stream of cars, the trees blurring in the golden light of the setting sun, shadows dancing across the windshield.

As the miles rolled by, I heard him lightly singing along to the music, and I realized that sometimes, silence was its own form of communication. And in that moment, it was exactly what we both needed.

Chapter Fifteen

The Hockey Game

I t was a two-hour drive to Raleigh for the game, and the winter sun was setting as we pulled into the parking lot of a Thai restaurant near the arena. We sat at the bar to eat a quick dinner, surrounded by young professionals flirting and joking with friends, most of them in their twenties and thirties. I remembered the hopefulness I felt at that age, with new money from new jobs, wearing new clothes. The independence of living on my own without any significant responsibilities. I really thought things would be different for me.

James mentioned that he had traveled through Asia and had authentic Thai food in Thailand. He even taught me how to pronounce the dishes we were eating. I butchered the names but tried anyway.

With only fifteen minutes before the puck drop, I found myself eating quickly, worried we were running late.

The last time I'd been to a game was for my son's eighth birthday. I had bought the best tickets I could afford, which weren't very good. I hoped the thrill of a live game would make up for it, but the inconveniences stacked up and I ended up regretting it. Even the parking was expensive. We had to park so far away we took a shuttle from the back parking lot to the arena. When we finally got to our seats, we were so high up we were almost vertical, and my son was terrified. He white-knuckled the first period, but it was clear he wasn't enjoying himself and it wasn't going to get better. So, we left our seats and decided to walk the perimeter.

We circled the arena, peeking in at the game when we passed each opening. I bought him Dippin' Dots and we lingered in the entry when we heard cheers, watching the replay on the jumbotron. After the second period, we called it a night and took the shuttle back to the car. He slept the two-hour drive home, and I stared into the black night feeling like I'd wasted money and wasted time. He would have been happy to order pizza and watch TV at home. He didn't need or ask for these tickets. I had tried so hard and wasn't even giving him what he wanted. I created problems and made things worse every time I tried to do something special.

"What's the rush?" James asked, watching me inhale my dinner. "There's no hurry."

James paid the tab and held my jacket for me as I slipped my arms into the sleeves. I thanked him, appreciating how considerate he was. He opened the car door for me again, and we drove to the arena, taking a different route than I'd ever taken. He passed a line of cars and asked a parking attendant for directions to the VIP parking. VIP parking? The attendant pointed us away from the traffic. We were met with another attendant who pointed us toward the arena. We parked just four rows away from the arena.

I didn't know what to think. I tried to act normal.

The game was Hurricanes vs. Penguins, and I was rooting for the Penguins, proudly wearing my Penguins shirt. I grew up in a hockey family, so I was excited to be there. Hockey is the only sport I enjoy outside of my kids' teams. When we reached our seats, I realized it wasn't just our parking that was VIP, our seats were too. We had tables in front of our seats and a waitress. I had never even seen seats like this before. I was having a Pretty Woman moment, but I was more Melissa McCarthy than Julia Roberts.

When I'm nervous, I talk. Things just start coming out of my mouth that no one in their right mind would share on a first date.

"I feel like Julia Roberts with all this VIP everything happening, except I have sex for free. I mean, not that I'm offering. I mean, I'm not not offering, but that wasn't the point. I was just trying to say this is all really nice. Do you always do a hockey game like this?"

Oh my God. Help me.

"Would you like a drink?" James chuckled.

"Yes," I said. "All of them. But I don't drink."

"Would now be a good time to start?"

"Probably, but it will only make more of this happen." I gesticulated to indicate the loops of my mind.

"I like it," he smiled. "The real you."

He put me at ease even when I was embarrassed.

The game started, and as always, hockey's fast pace kept me on the edge of my seat. We chatted as much as anyone can during a game, our eyes glued to the action, our sentences interrupted by the occasional scream or groan in response to a play on the ice. The conversation picked up, and I learned that the reason James knew the arena and nearby restaurants so well was that he had season tickets. His friends did too, and they would often go as a group or give each other their tickets to share with others. Sometimes he went with his family, sometimes with friends, and occasionally with coworkers.

"Are your friends here now?" I asked, glancing around at the people nearby.

"No, they all gave their seats away for this game, it seems," he said, scanning the crowd. "I don't recognize anyone."

He had a group of guy friends he spent time with, and the wives all got along too, so they would sometimes hang out or even travel as couples. I wondered if they were all as fit and attractive as he was. I tried to suck in my stomach and wondered when I last did a sit-up.

He told me about his travels—he'd been to a lot of places, both personally and for work. He and his wife had flown across the country just to see a concert one of them liked. They'd visited Greece, Spain, Turkey, France. He spoke of international travel as if it was as ordinary as getting the mail.

Many of his stories included friends or coworkers, and many included his wife. He talked about it all very comfortably, even her. I might have been overthinking in the car. He seemed comfortable talking about her. I could tell from the way he spoke about her that she had been his true partner, his teammate. His stories were filled with warmth, respect, and gratitude. They had a real love story—lovers, partners, and friends.

I enjoyed listening, but when he turned to me and asked, "What about you? Where do you like to travel?" I drew a blank.

Travel?

The only travel I did was to visit family. I couldn't think of a vacation I'd taken just to see something or experience a place.

"I don't travel very much," I admitted. "When I do, it's usually to visit my parents in Pittsburgh or my brother and his family in Boston."

"You should take your kids somewhere," he suggested, as if it had never crossed my mind.

"Yeah, I guess I should," I agreed. If only it were that easy. Airfare, hotels, events, food—it all added up to thousands of dollars. Even driving to see family was more expensive than I could afford. I didn't want to admit that.

"I'll be right back," he said, standing up. "If the waitress comes by, can you get me another beer? I've got a tab going."

"Sure," I said.

As he walked away, I sat there, taking it all in...the arena, the VIP section, the effortless way James moved through this world. And me, still trying to figure out if I even belonged in it.

I sat in my seat, staring out at the ice and the crowd but feeling completely alone in the stadium. Look at all these people who can pay for these tickets and have fun. I calculated and recalculated my finances. I had a decent-paying job. I didn't spend much, so where was it all going? I didn't color my hair, didn't drive a fancy car, didn't go on vacations. I had debt, sure, but by now, I should have made a dent in it, right? Why didn't I ever have enough? And then I remembered the answer. It was more surprising that I always seemed to forget it. I was doing everything on my own. I was the one paying the mortgage, keeping the car running, covering every little repair. I paid for three cell phones, clothing, sports. The bills stacked up, and there was no one to share them with.

And not just that, but I did the laundry, mowed the lawn, unloaded and loaded the dishes. I opened the mail, answered the door, scheduled the haircuts and dentist appointments. Every minute was booked and double booked.

While James was gone, I looked around at the stadium full of people cheering, laughing, carefree. Why couldn't I be like that? Why couldn't I just have fun and enjoy myself?

The envy I felt at the perceived ease of others, like James and his late wife, twisted into a tight knot in my gut, then quickly turned to self-pity. I was so tired of constant vigilance, drained from the never-ending survival mode.

I was so tired of my life. And now, here I was on a date at a hockey game with a handsome, considerate man, and I couldn't even enjoy it because it just reminded me of all the nights I sat at home trying to figure out how to pay a bill.

Instead of reminding myself to just enjoy the moment, I doubled down on myself, now criticizing and judging myself for these feelings. How self-absorbed of me! Here, he'd lost his soulmate and was still trying to give me a memorable evening, and I couldn't stop crying over my car payments. What kind of person did that make me?

The noise of the arena came rushing back as James returned. The crowd rose to their feet cheering. The Hurricanes had scored. "Woo hoo!" he cheered, eyes glued to the replay. He wasn't even a Hurricanes fan. We were there to root for the Penguins. But there he was, finding joy in the moment regardless of which team was winning. And just like that, I managed to blink away the tears before he could see me unraveling.

Chapter Sixteen

At Home

"It was awful," I told my cousin that night when I got home. "Not the date. The date was nice. James was amazing, but I was a party pooper. He had all these amazing experiences to share. He's traveled all over. He's met interesting people. I was so jealous, I couldn't even enjoy hearing them. It just made me think of everything I've never been able to do."

"I mean..." she started.

"And don't tell me how his life isn't perfect either because he lost his wife. I know that! That makes me feel even more stupid and self-absorbed to be crying over my bills when his soulmate is dead."

Jae was quiet. Even when I was wrong, she always listened to me with compassion.

"I'm just so tired of being here. I'm so sick of this life. Don't freak out. I'm not going to *do* anything, but if something happened to me, I wouldn't be mad. Give my kids the life insurance and sprinkle my dust in the garden."

Despite everything, I was grateful to have her. She listened to me being pathetic and dramatic and didn't judge me. She let me get it off my chest.

"Just keep praying," she said.

Comfort and clarity, comfort and clarity. I'd prayed for it so many times. I got on my knees to pray again with her reminder. I wanted to be freed from these patterns. I knew God could free me. I needed to give him my pain, in complete surrender.

Despite all the pain of my relationship with Gunther, the suffering had strengthened my relationship with God. I often thought about the moment I heard God's voice reminding me to turn to Him. He'd heard my prayer. He was there. I knew it in my heart. The pain had brought me closer to Him and that was a blessing. "Thank you for the suffering because it brings me closer to you," I added to my prayer when I felt brave. Each time I really thought I was at my bottom, my relationship with God got stronger.

While my eyes were closed in prayer, I heard a commotion in my backyard. The chickens were squealing, but it was too late at night. They should be asleep. I put on my headlamp and headed out back to see what was going on.

When I went outside, there was a giant raccoon climbing up the side of their big coop. He'd dug his way into their run, which was stapled to the side of the coop, and he couldn't get out. He turned and looked at me, his predatory eyes beaming bright gold in the light of my headlamp. My dog was quick behind me, bounding out barking aggressively. The raccoon snapped into action, remembered how he entered, and ran out the back.

I knew he'd be back. Now that he knew where he could find food, he'd be planning a more successful attempt. I trudged to my garage in my boots over my pajamas to grab a giant trap I had for raccoons. He wasn't the first I'd encountered. I dragged it out of the garage and set it near the hole he'd dug.

Before I went back inside, I looked up at the clear night sky. I sure did love to look up at the stars and wonder what was going on up there. When I got back inside, I went to put my phone on the charger and saw a text from Jae.

"I can't manifest for myself, but maybe I can manifest for you. I added you to my manifesting journal."

"Awesome. Thank you," I texted back without really knowing what a manifesting journal was. All I knew was she loved me, and I was lucky to have a single person that gave a shit about me.

Chapter Seventeen

The Website

There was no raccoon in the trap the next morning, but it didn't matter. All my chickens were safe and content, clucking softly as they pecked at the ground. I filled in the hole the raccoon had dug and repaired the fencing it had ripped apart. My dog watched me, occasionally chasing a squirrel before settling back down on the dead winter grass. The air was chilly, but the work kept me warm, moving and fixing things in the crisp morning.

Afterwards, I went inside to shower and make some food. As I was cooking, my phone dinged a sound I hadn't heard in a long time but recognized instantly. It was Gunther.

"No way," I thought, my heart skipping a beat. I didn't even want to see what he had to say. Things were finally going well, and except for my emotional breakdown last night, I was holding it together. Why now?

I picked up my phone and read his text. It said "Hey." Nothing else.

I took a screenshot of the text. It was the only message in an empty thread since I'd deleted our entire conversation history and his contact information from my phone. Yet somehow, his number was still linked to the special notification ding I'd created for him years ago. I sent the screenshot to Jae.

"No way," she texted back almost instantly. My phone started ringing. She was calling.

"What does he want?" she asked, her voice a mix of curiosity and concern.

"I don't know. I haven't replied."

"Are you going to?"

"No. Of course not. I'm doing great. Why would I ruin my progress?"

I'm not sure if either of us were convinced. I wanted to believe what I was saying.

"I swear he knows when you're starting to feel better. How do they always know? It's like they have this sixth sense. They all come back right when you're about to heal." she said.

"Every time," I agreed.

We hung up, but I couldn't shake the thoughts swirling in my head. Did he miss me? Was he regretting how things ended? If he was truly remorseful, would I even consider going back? Would I give it another try? My mind started wandering to what that might look like—mutual respect, better communication, him acknowledging my needs instead of shutting down and getting angry. A flicker of excitement and anticipation stirred within me. I had grown so much since then. Maybe things would be different this time.

Then another text came through: "Can you still make that website for me?"

The bubble of hope burst. I'd promised him I'd build a website for his business. He had said he was going to pay me. I wondered if he would still agree to that. I needed the money. He needed a website.

I replied, "Will you pay me?"

I waited and there was no response. I hated when he did this. He would initiate a conversation, get my attention and then disappear.

I texted again. "Do you have all the photos and text ready?"

"Yes, I'll pay you."

"Okay, I can do it next week."

"Great."

Shit. Shit. Shit.

At my next appointment, I told Natalie, "Gunther texted me."

"How did that go?" she asked, tilting her head slightly, her tone neutral but interested.

"Okay, I guess. Before we broke up, I was supposed to create a website for his main business. I'd already made one for the farm, and he liked it, so he wanted one for his other venture."

"Are you going to do it?" she asked.

"He said he'd pay me."

"Well, that sounds fair."

"One thousand five hundred," I said.

"Is that a good price?"

"It's a bargain for him. I'm sure he'd have to pay much more if he went somewhere else, but it's fair to me."

"Just don't sell yourself short," she advised.

"I won't."

Jae, of course, was more cautious.

"I bet he won't pay you," she had said. "He'll come up with some excuse."

"He's a bad boyfriend, but a good businessman," I told her. "I'm sure he'll pay."

"We'll see," she said, her skepticism clear.

Chapter Eighteen

Are We Dating?

The following week, James sent me funny memes during the day and called me after work. He made me laugh and made me feel like sharing. He asked what I liked to eat, what music I listened to. We talked about books, and I told him one of my favorite books was *Women* by Charles Bukowski, mostly because I loved the character, Lydia Vance.

To my surprise, James downloaded the book and said he was going to read it. I immediately regretted telling him how much I loved Lydia. What was he going to think? I felt exposed.

Lydia wasn't the kind of character most women would proudly admit to loving. She was wild, volatile, and fiercely sexual. She said everything she thought, felt everything she felt, and never looked back.

She didn't filter her emotions or worry about how she might be perceived. When she lost her shit over Henry Chinaski's terrible behavior, I didn't blame her. I rooted for her.

She was out of control and completely true to herself, all at once. Deep down, I wanted that kind of freedom. I wanted to feel everything, say everything, and not give a damn who couldn't handle it!

The next week, James asked me to go to dinner and a comedy club. These were actual dates. We were dating. Were we dating?

"Am I dating him?" I asked Natalie. "I mean, what is going on? He keeps asking me out but how do I know if he likes me?"

"If he keeps asking you out, then he likes you."

"Okay, yeah that sounds obvious, but also, it's not that obvious."

"Just go with the flow," she said. "He seems like a great guy."

"They all do at the beginning," I said.

"Just see what happens," she said.

The next week, his daughter was going to be spending the night at a friend's house.

"Do you want to stay over?" he asked. Of course, I wanted to.

His home was spacious and modern, but it lacked warmth, like a beautifully curated museum rather than a lived-in space. There were a few photos of him with his late wife on the bookshelf, but the house was otherwise devoid of personal touches, either feminine or masculine. It was immaculate, but eerily impersonal. Where were the piles of projects and messes?

We watched a movie on the oversized sectional in the living room with cathedral ceilings. He had a few drinks and got loose and handsy. I couldn't read him. Was he nervous? Was he drunk? Was this the first time he'd been with someone since she passed?

We made out on the couch, then moved to the guest bedroom. Between exploring each other's bodies, we shared our sexual preferences and boundaries, a tentative dance of trust. His fitness routine gave him stamina, and alcohol made him bold. I found myself responding to his advances eagerly, curious about him, wanting to know more.

We exchanged funny stories about our younger years, the wild things we did or wanted to do, the kind of stories you wouldn't share with just anyone. It felt like we were building something, laying the foundation for something deeper. Our bodies matched nicely; we took our time with each other, kissed, laughed and stayed up far too late.

When we finally decided to give each other a rest, I couldn't sleep. My mind was racing, unable to settle. His dogs roamed the house all night, their nails clicking on the wooden floors like a relentless metronome. In the middle of the night, thinking I was asleep, James slipped upstairs to his bedroom, returning with his pillow, blanket, and an eye mask. He couldn't sleep either. Even though we were in his house, we were both in an unfamiliar bed. We were in the guest room. His bed was upstairs. *Their* bed was upstairs.

In the morning, he got nervous his daughter would come home early and find me at his house. He might be ready to move on, but his daughter wasn't. She'd been through a lot losing her mother and he didn't want to upset her. Achy and exhausted, I was happy to leave so I could finally get some sleep.

That night, James left for a business trip. He had meetings and conferences the beginning of the week then he was going to meet up with friends in Las Vegas before returning home. He would be gone over a week.

I buried myself in schoolwork and when I needed a break from that, I worked on Gunther's website. I was taking Business Law with a professor who seemed determined to have us read the entire history of law. We had weekly tests that required not only understanding the case law but also applying the theory to real-life scenarios. As soon as my workday ended, I'd open my iPad and laptop to study for class. When I was too burnt out from homework to think, I'd shift to updating landing pages and menus, editing photos and writing text for Gunther's website.

Even though I was uncomfortable with the lack of communication from James, I didn't have time to overthink. I had to make sense of Miranda v. Arizona, Brown v. Board of Education and Marbury v. Madison.

At therapy, I told Natalie about my concerns.

"I've hardly heard from him. He left end of last week for conferences then went on a boy's trip."

"Sounds like he's got a lot going on," Natalie tried to reassure me.

"He only sent a couple of texts the entire week he was gone and took hours to respond to mine. He would text me, I would immediately answer, and then I'd get nothing back."

Something didn't feel right. Was it too soon to be intimate? Was he having second thoughts? Maybe I was being needy. Then again, maybe he'd lost interest. I had so many questions I didn't even want to ask out loud.

"Just focus on your schoolwork and try not to think about it," Natalie said.

"Do you think it's weird I haven't heard from him?"

"We don't know if it's suspicious or not," she said. "Has he given you any reason to be suspicious?"

"I mean, this is suspicious."

"Not necessarily. It suggests you have different needs as far as communication. That can be negotiated. Not every man is going to lie to you, Kathryn."

"Okay," I agreed, but I didn't believe her. This felt all too familiar. The strong interest leading up to sexual intimacy then the shift in attention.

"Talk to him when he gets back. You can ask him if this is the level of communication to expect when he travels, and if it's not enough for you, you can ask him to communicate more frequently."

"Okay." That sounded reasonable. She was a professional. I should listen to her.

When I knew James was back in town I called. He had a minute to chat before getting dinner together. I didn't want to bombard him right away with my concerns but also needed to get it off my chest.

"The business meetings were pretty grueling," he said. "There wasn't much time for texting or calls. Long dinners after the meetings."

"Okay," I said. "I understand."

"I've got to run," he said. "We'll get together soon."

I didn't feel good about any of this. It was hard to believe there was that little time, but I didn't want to let my insecurities get in the way of something good. Natalie said not every man is going to lie to me. I really wanted to believe that.

That night I finished the website for Gunther and emailed him all the files and passwords. I felt good about the work I'd done and was pleased I was able to complete the work without ever having to talk to him on the phone or see him in person.

There was no opportunity to argue, we didn't address anything personal. It was completely professional. I sent him an invoice for $1,500. The thought of being able to deposit that check and put it toward my credit card was so satisfying. I started to wonder if I could make some more websites. I wrote up a pitch to send to a couple other people I knew who had small businesses with lackluster websites. Maybe things were turning around.

Chapter Nineteen

Touring Colleges

College acceptance letters began to trickle in for my daughter, Eliza. She anxiously awaited news from her first-choice school, but in the meantime, she received a quick acceptance into the engineering program at her second choice.

Eliza had always been ambitious and thoughtful in her planning. Her careful approach to the college application process reflected her personality - meticulous, forward-thinking, and determined. Though she was grateful for the acceptance, I knew she was still holding out hope for her first choice.

Any school that accepted her would be lucky to have her. Even amid her own anxieties, she maintained her sensitivity to others. She had a strong sense of what was right, always including others and making sure no one felt left out. This thoughtfulness was evident even as a young child. I used to take her and her younger brother to Chick-Fil-A for a quick bite to eat in the rushed space between Saturday activities. While I nursed her baby brother, she loved to go down the slide in the playroom. More times than I can count, she would encounter a child who wanted to slide down but was afraid to do it alone. Eliza would offer to go down with them, holding them in her arms. The delight and relief on both their faces as they emerged at the bottom of the slide made my heart beam with love and pride.

Her character was unchanged, even as she faced her own challenges. She is a cheerleader for others, a connector, and an organizer. I knew that going to the school that felt like a the right fit was important to her. She worked hard. She was dedicated. I wanted her to be recognized for her talents.

I watched Eliza taking notes during the tour, asking thoughtful questions, introducing herself to other prospective students. I recognized the complex emotions she was navigating, the tension between practicality and desire, between gratitude and disappointment. This struggle mirrored so many others in her life, especially the big one I had created: my divorce from her dad. She and her brother had lived out of suitcases, meetings with parenting coordinators, parking lot drop offs, and legal documents. Yet she never gave up her kindness despite the hurt. I admired her resilience even as I wished she didn't have to be quite so strong so young.

The news of her first acceptance letter brought a blend of relief and anticipation, though part of me remained preoccupied with the silence from James.

I wasn't sure if I was "having too many expectations" like I had with Gunther, or if there was something he wasn't saying. I found myself dissecting every interaction, or lack thereof, with a growing sense of unease.

Finally, I decided to send him a text. I typed, deleted and retyped. "I'm taking my daughter to Charlotte to tour the campus. We're leaving early Friday, heading back Saturday. Just wanted to let you know in case you're around this weekend."

His response came later: "I'll take you to dinner when you get back."

Maybe everything was fine. Maybe I was just overthinking.

Eliza and I met up with my parents in Charlotte for the campus tour. They drove from Pittsburgh. It was an opportunity to see us, support their granddaughter and see the school. It was a five-hour drive from Wilmington for me, and seven hours from Pittsburgh for them, a decent compromise for meeting in the middle.

I always invited my parents to join us on these trips. We got along well which I was grateful for. Despite my frustrations, I knew I was tremendously lucky to have a wonderful family that loved me. Our relationship had matured over the years, evolving from the turbulent parent-teen dynamic to a friendship I deeply valued. They'd supported me through countless challenges, and I was grateful for their unwavering presence in my life, even if they were far away.

While I genuinely wanted to spend time with them, there was another, more shameful reason for inviting them: I was out of money. I barely had enough to cover gas to Charlotte. I knew there was a strong possibility that my dad would pick up the tab for food and the hotel room. My credit cards were maxed out, and even if I tried to charge something, it would be declined. I was too embarrassed to ask.

I despised my financial situation but was determined to hide the severity of it from my kids, my parents and everyone else. When things got particularly tight, I'd even borrow money from my kids' savings, only to sneak it back into their account before anyone noticed.

My mother, a bright, inquisitive, and creative intellectual, had devoted her life to higher education and community service. It was her passion. My father, warm, generous, and always quick with a joke, adored my mother and my kids. He was one of the few men I'd met who I'd truly consider a feminist—always encouraging women to express themselves and reach their fullest potential.

By all indications, I had all the privilege, support and opportunity to be a thriving success, yet I was failing.

In my mind I just needed to hold things together long enough to get my kids off to a good start in adulthood, and then I'd turn things around. I'd do anything necessary. I'd work three jobs. I would sell the house, pay off my debt, live in my car, and start over. Maybe I'd get a better job. Maybe a promotion. I wasn't where I wanted to be, but I was on the right path—or so I kept telling myself.

The college tour went as expected. The campus was beautiful, the students lively and full of energy. I could see the desperate attempt to fall in love with this campus in her eyes, even though it was clear, she'd had her heart set on State.

I didn't want my kids to have to learn how to fake joy during disappointment. They worked hard. I wanted them to see results. I wanted them to receive the rewards their hard work, integrity and heart deserved.

We all had breakfast together Saturday before heading home. My Dad excused himself while my mom and I finished our coffee.

When we went up to get our bags in the room, my dad was returning. "I covered your room," he said casually.

"Thank you," I replied, trying to mask the deep mix of shame and gratitude I felt. My daughter and mother were right behind me, ready to head out. As we rolled our bags to the car, I turned to my daughter with a familiar, dark joke. "Remember, I've got life insurance. Just off me by 59, and you'll be set—all your college loans paid off, and then some."

It was a joke I'd made too many times to count, but this time it felt different. My eyes burned as the weight of my words settled in. I wasn't joking.

Chapter Twenty

Another Date

By the time I'd dropped my daughter off at her dad's house, got home and showered, the weather had turned to rain. It was the kind of rain that was heavy and drenching. Water quickly pooled up in the streets. It was impossible to go even the short distance from the house to the car without getting completely soaked.

After all the driving, I wanted to relax into the evening. James was spending time with me. He'd bought me dinner. I needed to trust the process. He was casual. I wanted to be casual and relaxed too, but I remembered that Natalie said I should talk to him about his level of communication. I started to say something and then changing my mind. I was afraid it would come out wrong.

"Is something wrong?" he asked.

"No, I'm fine. I'm just totally fine. I'm just eating." Now I was being weird. "Well, I was going to say some... no, I'm fine. How was your trip?" Then, without self-restraint, "You just fell off the face of the earth there. I thought I was never going to hear from you again."

"Woah, woah what?" he was confused. "Why would you never hear from me again?"

"I just figured you were ghosting me. We had sex, then you went on a trip, then I didn't hear from you for almost a week. That's when the ghosting happens so I just figured..."

"Woah, no one's ghosting anyone. That's so rude."

"Yeah," my heart was racing. We were standing in his kitchen eating at the island and the food kept falling off my fork back into my food right when I was about to put it in my mouth.

"Need some help?" he asked playfully.

I was determined to get my sentence out. I stabbed my food hard with the fork. "I just didn't hear from you, so..."

"I get it," he interrupted. "I was really tied up in the meetings and then when I got to Vegas, we all put our phones in the safe. That's our agreement, you know so we can have quality time.

"Right," I said. "For the boys weekend."

"We don't get together often, so we try to make the most of it."

"Right."

"You don't sound like you believe me."

"I believe you." I lied. I didn't believe him, but I wanted to.

We went to the couch to watch a movie. His daughter was spending the night with a friend again.

"Do you want to go upstairs?" he asked, with a grin. He was very handsome, with a warm smile and confident eyes. He left no room for doubt that he desired me sexually.

"Of course!"

We hopped up from the couch and started to head upstairs.

"We can go in the guest room if that's better," I offered. "It doesn't bother me."

"I'm ready," he said. "Let's go."

Though part of me wondered if this was a meaningful shift, I wasn't about to question his comfort level. If he was ready to bring me into *their* bedroom, that was entirely up to him.

There was a landing at the top of the stairs and a doorway to the bedroom. The bed was to the left and his bedroom was so large it had a separate sitting area with two reading chairs and a lamp. I barely had a moment to look around before he was pulling my shirt up over my head and inching my pants down over my hips. He unfastened his belt and unbuttoned his pants, and they slid down to his ankles. He stepped out of them and walked me backwards with his arm around my back and laid me down on the bed. He kissed my breasts, my stomach, my hips and started to spread my legs apart.

Then his phone buzzed. He stood up suddenly and looked at it.

"She's coming home," he said.

"Who is?" I asked, confused.

"My daughter. She just texted she's not feeling well, she's coming home." He pulled up her location. "She's twenty minutes away."

"I can leave," I said.

"Not yet," he said. He pushed me back on the bed and climbed on top of me. The urgency of his desire and the heat of his lust and release was exciting. My heart was racing and I let myself completely give in to the moment.

My confidence in being able to keep things casual was shot. How could I remain detached after being ravaged under a skylight in the pouring rain by a sexy man with a playful smile, a chiseled body, and a love of reading?

We caught our breath for only a moment, then he hopped up.

"I feel like a teenager hiding from my parents," he said. "But I'm the parent, sneaking around my teenager."

I put my clothes back on quickly. I was smiling. He was right. There was a thrill to getting away with something, indulging in something together, being sneaky, being sexy.

"Text me when you get home," he said, giving me one last kiss on the lips.

Chapter Twenty-One

The Dream

When I got home, I jumped in the shower one more time then crawled into bed. I decided to turn my alarm off so I could wake up naturally, a rare indulgence. There wasn't anything urgent going on the next day. I was a couple weeks into my next class and tomorrow was the Superbowl. Superbowl Sunday was always a nice, quiet day for me since I wasn't into sports.

After I turned my alarm off, I opened social media to scroll for a bit. The first thing to pop up was a photo on James' feed. He'd posted it four days earlier but it hadn't shown up on my feed until now. It was a picture of a concert. The lighting was orange and gold, and the crowd filled a stadium. That's strange, he said he didn't have his phone in Vegas. My throat closed as that familiar feeling returned that what I was told did not match what I was seeing. It felt like Gunther all over. The social media telling a different story, a life of secrets. Me the fool.

This time, though, I wasn't in love with him. It hadn't gotten that far. The memory of letting myself surrender to him completely with the rain pelting the sky light, and his tongue deep in my mouth made me wonder if I was lying to myself. But the steadiness of my heart reassured me that there was truth in my assessment. I was keeping my head on straight for the most part. And with this new information, I might pull back even farther.

I fell asleep believing what I was telling myself, which was better than crying. It was Saturday February 11, 2023. The next day was the Super Bowl.

I woke up in the middle of the night, jolted from a vivid and active dream. I was mad I'd woken up. I wanted to go right back to sleep and keep dreaming the dream. It felt so real and vivid. I was with James and his late wife, but she was my best friend in the dream. She was so friendly and fun. She didn't speak in words, but she giggled, and I knew what she was saying. Her giggles were like music, like she was singing. She was showing me around. We would be in one place and in an instant, we would be states away somewhere else. She was taking me all over the country, showing me all the things she loved, all the places she'd been.

When I couldn't fall back asleep, I decided to hold onto the dream by writing it down. The dream felt important. It wasn't just interesting or inspiring. It wasn't just ideas. It was feelings. It felt real.

I wrote down everything I could remember. I was afraid it would be completely incoherent in the morning but kept adding whatever I remembered. It was several pages long.

Chapter Twenty-Two

Don't Tell Him

The next morning, I called Jae and told her about the dream.

"It was so strange," I began. "We were in James's guest room, and his sister was there. She was upset about something. I got the sense she was dealing with some personal drama or trauma. She seemed distressed, like she was struggling, and James couldn't help, which only frustrated her more. Then she left. That was the only part of the dream that felt bad."

"After that, James and I went to this café that was also a hospital. You could order treatments from a menu written in chalk on a chalkboard, like if you were ordering a smoothie. We were looking at this big menu written in pretty colors to order some treatment for him. That's when Julie appeared. But she wasn't there for him, she was there for me. She came so she could show me around while we left him there to get his treatment. The doctor asked me to choose the treatment from the chalk menu. I thought his wife should decide but she was like "pick anything!" She just reassured me that James would be fine and that I was making the right choice."

"What treatment did he need?" Jae asked.

"I don't remember exactly. It didn't seem serious like a surgery or anything. It was like deep rest and healing. But that part was fuzzy. I just knew he was there for something that would take a while and so his wife and I could leave and come back. His wife told me he needed to go through some things but that he would be okay. She wanted me to leave him there with the doctor."

"So, did you leave?"

"Yeah, we left him there and then she took me on a tour of some of her favorite things: a car, a house. She was giggling the whole time, and her giggles sounded almost like she was singing. She was so excited to be with me, like we were old friends who hadn't seen each other in years. It felt like it does when you're just picking up right where you left off. Like us, but happy."

She laughed. "Sounds nice. What did she tell you?"

"She kept telling me that everything would be okay. She said she liked my laugh, and it felt like the most sincere and genuine compliment I've ever received. It was like she was complimenting my soul. She said James needed to go through some things, but he would be fine. And she told me that I would be okay. It didn't feel like a platitude; it felt like she knew what she was talking about. It felt like fact. Everything will be okay. I believed her."

"Was there anything else?"

"I feel like I still believe her. I feel really calm and content today."

"I want that feeling," she said.

"I can't blame you."

"Anything else?"

"She wanted to go swimming, so we went into the ocean together. We swam and played in the waves. We were jumping over the waves and diving back into the water. When I looked over at her I saw that she was a dolphin and then I saw myself and I was a dolphin too."

"Wow."

"That's it."

"That's a lot."

"I kind of want to tell him about it, but is that weird? I mean, it's pretty random, and I'm sure he doesn't care about my dreams, but for some reason, I really want to tell him."

"He might take it wrong," Jae advised.

"Too much information?"

"Definitely oversharing. And it's about his dead wife. That's pretty weird. He might think you are trying to create some false sense of intimacy."

"Ohh that would not be good." I did not want him to think that. I agreed not to say anything. I would just keep it to myself. I was always saying things out of nowhere, oversharing and I thought it bored people. It definitely pushed people away. I needed to learn how to keep my mouth shut. Having the conversation with Jae gave me the presence of mind to show some restraint.

Chapter Twenty-Three

Super Bowl Sunday

James was going to stop by before heading off to watch the Superbowl with friends. I knew I had one goal: Don't tell him about the dream. He could take it the wrong way. It was really weird. I didn't want him to think I was weird or manipulating him. It was a sensitive subject to him, he'd lost his wife. Definitely not something to casually bring up.

When James arrived, he was dressed in jeans and a t-shirt, holding a Yeti cup filled with a cocktail. I heard the ice clinking against the metal sides as he set the cup on my counter before pulling me into a hug. There was an easy confidence about him, as if life always went his way. I had to remind myself that his life wasn't perfect, he'd lost his wife, his soulmate.

"Funniest thing," I blurted out. "I had a dream about your late wife last night."

I was more surprised than he was by what I'd just said. How did that come out? I was determined not to bring it up. Sometimes I really hated being me.

"You did?" He seemed curious.

I tried to backpedal. "How did you sleep? Do you dream?"

"What was the dream about?" he asked.

"I mean, I don't know. It was all over the place. But she was really nice in the dream. She said she liked my laugh."

I could feel the weight of his gaze. I tried to steer the conversation away, but I was already trapped by my own words.

"What else happened?" he pressed.

"It was really weird. Are you sure you want to hear?"

"Yes," he said, taking the dream very seriously.

"Well, it started at your house. Your sister was there too."

"My sister?"

"At least in my dream you had a sister."

"I do have a sister."

"Huh, I guess you must have told me that."

He interrupted, "No, I don't think I would have mentioned her."

I was feeling increasingly self-conscious. He probably thinks I'm snooping on him.

"Tell me more," he urged, his interest piqued.

Now I worried he'd be disappointed by the dream. "She was really friendly. She was so outgoing and warm. She treated me like I was her best friend. She said she liked my laugh. Her voice sounded like music. You were there, but then she and I went to the ocean. We turned into dolphins and jumped the waves."

I studied his reaction. His expression revealed nothing. "Weird, I know."

"I think she would have liked you," he said quietly.

"I wrote it all down," I confessed before I could stop myself.

"Can I see it?"

"Sure." I grabbed my notebook from my bedside table and handed it to him. It was still open to the section I had written.

The awkward silence that followed felt like an eternity. I regretted saying anything. I wished I'd listened to Jae. I wished I knew how to keep my mouth shut.

Finally, he handed the notebook back to me and said something that would change my perspective on life forever. "Are you sure it was a dream?" he asked.

I was taken aback. "What else would it be?" I asked him.

"Do you usually have dreams like this? And write them out for pages?"

"Not often, but I've done it before. Not exactly like this but sometimes I get ideas when I'm falling asleep."

"Why did you write this one down?"

"I just felt like I needed to," I explained, still unable to read his reaction. "I felt like I needed to for you, but that doesn't make any sense."

"It does make sense," he said.

"Really?"

He asked me again, "Are you sure it was a dream?"

My mind was spinning. I hated this feeling. I had no idea what he was implying and felt like no matter what I said, I would be wrong. Did he think I made it up? I braced myself for an accusation.

After so many years of being misunderstood and misinterpreted, I felt defensive and confused. I tried to quiet my racing thoughts.

"What else would it be?" I looked at him with suspicion.

"It could have been a visitation," he explained.

"What is that?"

"You haven't heard of a visitation?"

"No." I had no idea what he was talking about.

"It's when someone who is dead comes to visit in a dream. They give messages and comfort. It's a way for people on the other side to communicate with us here. It's a visit from their soul. It feels real because it is real. That was really Julie."

I was trying to process what he was telling me. Dead people communicating with living people? In my sleep? What he was telling me now was far more bizarre than anything I'd ever said. Far more bizarre even than my random dream.

"She's visited two other people recently," he continued. "You're the third. Their dreams were a lot like yours."

"Like a ghost? Is she a ghost?"

"I don't know how it works," he admitted.

"Why me, though? Why wouldn't she just visit you?"

He shrugged. He looked tense.

"She seems to have an easier time communicating with women," he said. "Women are more spiritually open. Maybe you're just really open and she knew she could get through to you."

I could feel his sorrow. There was so much stillness between us.

"If you have another dream, let me know. I think she's trying to tell me something."

He picked up his Yeti, gave me a one-armed squeeze and left through the back door.

Chapter Twenty-Four

Why Me?

In the days following the visitation dream, I felt disoriented. I'd go through my usual routine, then suddenly pause and replay the dream in my mind to reassure myself that it had really happened, that it wasn't something I'd imagined. I found articles online about visitation dreams and read them over and over. I combed through my notes from the dream, trying to make sense of it all.

All I could think about was how crazy this all sounded. Everything I believed in was being challenged. How could she be dead but not dead? Was she or wasn't she a ghost? If she was a ghost, why wasn't she trying to scare me? Was she going to haunt me? If we aren't really dead, then what are we? And if we are something else, then *where* are we? I had no reference point to make sense of any of this.

My belief system was simple: life was biological. We're here, and then we're gone. I understood the concept of heaven and hell, but if I were completely honest, I believed that when we died, we just stopped living. Poof. The end.

I didn't see heaven as a reward or hell as a punishment; I believed we did the right thing because of our moral compass. Doing the wrong thing, even if never discovered, could mentally torture us. In fact, if there was a hell, this must already be it.

The information I found online was conflicting. Some articles described visitation dreams as real and common events where a family member or ancestor visits the living with a message of healing, guidance, or warning. They claimed that these dreams had been happening throughout history. Other sources, however, dismissed them as a product of the mind, a way to process grief and loss using memories of the deceased.

But that didn't explain my experience. I had no memories of her. I wasn't grieving. I had never even met her. All I knew was that she had passed away and had a husband who happened to be incredibly attractive, thoughtful and fun. None of the articles mentioned visitation dreams involving someone you never even met.

As tempting as it was to spend all my free time contemplating the meaning of life and what happens after death, I had pressing responsibilities. I needed to maintain a B average to keep my tuition covered by my employer. Weekly closed-book quizzes and a looming final exam demanded my attention. I should have been focusing on legal cases and concepts like personal liability, strict liability, negligence, and fraudulent misrepresentation.

Instead, my mind was consumed with existential questions: What if we don't really die when we die? What if we continue to exist and can still interact with people? What else can we do? And why had she visited me instead of her own husband? The questions were endless. I could turn the possibilities over in my mind a million times, but one thing I couldn't do was deny the experience of the dream.

I just felt different. The sense of peace she had given me when she said everything would be okay lingered. I believed her. Not just with my mind, but with my heart. My mind could still analyze it, argue with it, and rationalize it away, but my heart believed she was right: everything was going to be okay. I was going to be okay.

"They're real," Jae said when I asked her. "I've had them with my sister."

"Why am I the last person on earth to hear about this kind of thing?"

"I don't know, it just never came up."

Perhaps it hadn't come up because there was never a need. Jae had lost her sister and both her parents. She was intimately familiar with grief and loss. In contrast, my parents were still alive and well, as was my brother. The people I'd lost were either not that close to me or had lived long, fulfilling lives. Their passing was expected and unremarkable.

"Funny," Jae added wryly, "how after all these years of wanting to feel reassured, seen, and comforted in a relationship, you finally get it, but it's from a dead woman."

We both erupted into laughter. Her comedic timing was brutal and perfect.

There's an aspect of dissociation that happens when we are struggling. Maybe it's a necessary survival skill. We know we are suffering, we feel the suffering, but we are simultaneously forced to get on with the routine of living. We have responsibilities that prevent the hours of weeping we'd like to indulge in. We deny ourselves the full awareness of our suffering because we have to eat, work, put gas in the car. I knew I was struggling, but didn't know how heavy it was until it lifted.

When I shared my research on visitation dreams and my lingering questions with James, he suggested that perhaps I was more spiritually open than most people, making me a suitable conduit for his wife's messages. He confessed he'd gone to a few mediums in the months after her passing. He'd read spiritual books trying to find peace and closure to help him with her unexpected death.

It surprised me that James would go to a medium. James was very level-headed. He had served in the military, and worked in a corporate environment. To me, mediums were make-believe. At best they were entertaining, at worst they were con artists preying on the vulnerable.

James believed. He said the medium had shared details about his wife that she couldn't have known otherwise. He even suggested that sometimes the deceased will help bring people together from the other side, guiding their loved ones toward happiness. Perhaps, he mused, his wife had recognized my open spirit and good heart and wanted us to meet.

I imagined her flying above the town, looking down at us all tucked into our beds, and spotting me, sprawled sideways, drool on my pillow, my head full of swirling nonsense. "That's the one!" She decided before nose diving into my awareness for a good old dream and a dolphin swim before checking in on her other friends.

I liked the idea that she saw something special in me that no one else had noticed. I secretly hoped she would visit me again. I wanted to know more about her, to discover if we truly would have been best friends.

Chapter Twenty-Five

Just a Quick Nap

James and I both had a free Saturday. Our respective kids were occupied with friends and their own interests, so we decided to spend the afternoon together at his house. To be honest, even though I loved my house, I was a little embarrassed by it. There were repairs I couldn't afford to make, floors that were worn and faded, and a carpet with no plush left after twenty years of wear.

I had a stain on my ceiling from when my AC overflowed five years ago and stains on my couch from the kids and the dog. One time when James was over, he casually mentioned that even a house can fall apart if you don't maintain it. He wasn't trying to be rude; he didn't know that my house wasn't entirely neglected. Things seemed to break faster than I could fix them. I could only put out the fires that were actively burning. The ones smoldering in the background would have to wait.

When I went to his house, he had me park under the trees by the street in the lot next to his instead of on his bright circular driveway or in the parking spots next to his garage. I drove a three-cylinder Mitsubishi Mirage stick shift that I loved because it got almost 45 miles per gallon and was fun to drive. There was nothing wrong with it. The paint was shiny, and it was only five years old. But it was a "cheap" car, and maybe I was a "cheap" woman. Maybe I was the kind of woman who needed to park away from the house, who he needed to "sneak in so the neighbors wouldn't see her."

I pushed those thoughts away. It didn't matter. I was going to change my situation eventually, and he was just a distraction. I knew that a better car would not make me a better person. I was already a good person.

It was one of those winter days that was chilly with a clear blue sky and a sun that beamed through his high windows. The light created strong heat directly where it poured in but nowhere else. His house was a little cold with all those high ceilings, tall windows and perfect walls. We curled up under a blanket on the couch, then decided to skip the movie and go straight upstairs to his bedroom for a Saturday afternoon nap.

The last time I was in his bedroom, his late wife had "followed me home." I wasn't even sleeping in his bed when I had the dream. I wondered if I would dream about her again. Would it be like last time? Would she still treat me like her best friend? The idea of going to sleep made me excited with the possibility of another visit. I'd never slept in HER bed. It felt almost guaranteed. I hoped I would fall asleep fast. I tempered my expectations and reminded myself it was just a quick nap. And, the dream was a one-time thing, right?

Their bedroom was bigger than my living room. If you included their enormous bathroom and closet, their bedroom was almost the size of my house. When James was in the bathroom, I peeked in her closet and noticed all her clothes were still hanging there. She had shoes upon shoes, purses, accessories, and belts. She had so many nice things. James came out of the bathroom and got in bed.

"I'll just be a minute," I said. I closed the bathroom door behind me.

Inside the bathroom, she had a huge vanity with makeup, many perfumes, and displays for necklaces, bracelets, and earrings. Everything was carefully organized and displayed. She had enough bracelets to go up both arms. The perfumes were name brand. I carefully picked one up to smell it.

"Are you trying to figure out the toilet?" James shouted from the bedroom. He startled me and I almost dropped the perfume onto all her perfect jewelry.

"It's a bidet!" he shouted again. I carefully put down the perfume and walked over to the toilet. I stared at it. I'd never seen a bidet before.

"You should use it!" he shouted. "It's the best! It's very sanitary! You'll love it!"

For some reason, I was afraid of the bidet. I imagined myself pressing the wrong lever, breaking something, flooding the bathroom, scrambling to hide the destruction, falling on the marble floor with my pants down, cracking my head open on the toilet bowl, and getting blood all over his perfect house.

I looked to see if he even had toilet paper. Do you even use toilet paper with a bidet? Do you use it first? After? Not at all? I had no idea what to do, but I wasn't going to ask a grown man to come into the bathroom and potty train me. There was toilet paper, so I wiped, stood up and prayed I was pressing the right handle to flush. I washed my hands and went back to the bedroom.

"Did you use the bidet?" James asked.

"Uh, no," I mumbled.

He chuckled. "It won't hurt you. You've got to try it sometime. Really, it's no big deal."

"Okay, yeah, absolutely, for sure, definitely next time," I lied.

He laughed again, "It's ok. Do what you want."

He wrapped his arms around me and pulled me up against him. His body was already so warm from the covers. I wondered what it was like to *be her*, living in that big house with James to sleep next to every night. He was the kind of man who took care of things like car maintenance, house repairs, and setting up electronics. He bought her jewelry, supported her dreams and didn't complain about all her clothes and shoes. He was everything a woman would want.

I looked out the bedroom window at the pale blue sky. In the distance, I could see the water. There was still some green on the trees. I looked at the trees and tried to find a bird among the many leaves and branches until I heard him quietly snoring, then I drifted off too.

Chapter Twenty-Six

The Weight of Grief

When I woke up, I was crying. It felt as if no time had passed at all, but nearly an hour had slipped by. The bright sunlight had faded, turning the sky an indigo blue, and the green leaves outside the window now looked black. Panic gripped me. I felt physically paralyzed, yet my heart was pounding so hard I could barely breathe. Pulling myself up to a sitting position felt like climbing out of a pit filled with lead.

"Are you okay?" James asked. He was only half awake.

I couldn't respond. I had to get out of there. I scrambled to find my shoes, considering for a moment just leaving them behind. I wasn't okay. I had to go home. I had to leave. I knew my behavior would be alarming, but I couldn't speak, and I didn't care. The only thought in my mind was escape.

He followed me downstairs to the front door, asking again, "Are you okay?"

I managed to squeak out, "I'll text you later," before jogging to my car and driving off. He stood in his doorway, confused.

Less than a mile away from his house, I pulled into a small neighborhood under arching trees, turned off the car, and leaned my head back to breathe. I was sobbing uncontrollably, unable to see through the tears flooding my eyes. I was too upset to drive safely, so I forced myself to stop until I could catch my breath.

I grabbed my phone and texted him: "I wish it was me that died instead of her."

"Why would you ever say something like that?" he replied.

"That's how I was feeling. You both had everything I ever wanted. I'm sorry you lost her. And I'm sorry she doesn't get to be here with you."

"Me too, and thank you, but nothing will bring her back."

I felt sick from head to toe. My head hurt, my heart hurt, my body hurt. I felt so heavy, like I was miles deep in the earth, trying to move through dirt instead of walking through air. Why was I alive? Why did I let myself get hopeful again? Why did I try to enjoy something? I should have known it wouldn't last! I am such a fool!

I drove the rest of the way home and crawled into bed to cry. I was in a pit of depression as deep as any I'd ever felt. I hated being here. I hated struggling for everything and never feeling like I was making any progress. I hated having to be "okay" and "doing fine" for the comfort of others. I hated getting punched in the gut every time I tried to be happy. I hated that I had to keep living this stupid life with all this suffering.

Here was a woman who was in love. They had money, ease, fun. They had a great sex life. They went on vacations together. They communicated and had shared hobbies. Why the fuck did God take her when he could have taken me, just a couple miles away, in my falling apart house, miserable, pathetic, worthless, and begging to go?

Chapter Twenty-Seven

Calling a Medium

I wasn't feeling much better the next day. Exhaustion weighed on me like a heavy blanket, and my thoughts were clouded with confusion and dread. I couldn't shake the feeling that somehow Julie was mad at me, punishing me for sleeping with her husband. If she could give me such a great dream, maybe she could give me a terrible one too. Except there was no dream to remember this time. I just woke up out of nothingness wanting to die.

I was in no position to spend money frivolously, but this felt like an emergency. If James believed in mediums, maybe I was wrong about them. After all, I used to think we just turned into nothing when we died, and now I was sure we didn't. Maybe I was wrong about mediums too and if they are real, maybe one can talk to Julie and ask her why she's mad at me.

I found a hotline that had psychics and mediums, promising five free minutes if I signed up. Every minute after that was another seven dollars. I had eighty dollars in my checking account to last the next four days. I hoped this would be quick.

I selected a psychic medium from the list named Monica and waited for the hotline to call me back. Within moments, my phone rang, and after a prompt, I accepted the call. When Monica joined, I spoke quickly, my words tumbling out in a rush.

Hearing myself explain the situation out loud, I felt incoherent and delusional. I hadn't told many people what was going on and speaking it out loud made me feel crazier than ever.

"I met this guy who's a widower, and one night after I slept with him, his late wife followed me home, and I had a dream about her. It was an amazing dream, and I felt so close to her, reassured, and comforted. I remembered every detail and wrote it all down for him. He said it was probably really her, and it was called a visitation dream. But today, I took a nap with him, and when I woke up, I felt hopeless and wanted to die. Is that her? Did she make me feel that way? Is she mad at me now? Does she wish I was dead?"

"Oh honey, slow down. It's not any of that. She's right here with me now."

I was stunned. Julie really got around! She's everywhere! I didn't understand yet that without a physical body, we can be anywhere and everywhere.

The medium continued, "Do you know that you are an empath? Do you know what that is?"

"I don't really know what it is, no."

"It means you are very empathetic."

"Oh, yeah, okay then. Yeah, I can put myself in other people's shoes."

"It's more than that. It means you can feel someone else's emotions as if they were your own."

"I'm not following."

"You weren't feeling her at all. She is very loving and high in spirits. You weren't feeling her; you were feeling his feelings. You were feeling his grief."

"His grief..."

"Grief is incredibly heavy. It's one of the heaviest, most dense energies. He is still feeling it. He has done all his grieving in that bed, and you picked it up from the energy of that space. You are a sponge."

Relief washed over me knowing she wasn't mad at me; I wasn't being punished for something. But I hadn't realized how deeply he was still grieving. He seemed so cheerful, confident, and agreeable. He hid it well. He was stronger than I was. I could barely handle my feelings, and I hadn't even lost someone. My problems felt small in comparison.

No wonder you hear stories about a husband or wife dying within days of their partner from a broken heart. If that's what grief feels like, I don't know how people continue to function.

"You need to learn how to protect your energy," Monica added.

Before I could ask more, an automated voice cut in, saying my time was up. Did I want to add more money to keep talking? Yes, yes, I did want to! But I had no money to add. I hung up and quickly wrote down everything she said.

While I was writing, I was thinking about that pit of despair, the heaviness of his grief. It felt insurmountable when I was under it. Catastrophic. And also, familiar. While I had never lost someone to death like James had, I'd lost people I loved to change. My heartbreak over Gunther felt heavy like that grief. I also felt that heaviness at the hockey game. In a way, I was grieving the life I wanted that felt out of reach. Maybe my experiences weren't exactly the same grief James was going through. Maybe mine were just *grief adjacent*. Maybe there were more subtle and nuanced kinds of grief than we realize. Maybe we need a word for each kind of grief the way Eskimo's have words for all the different kinds of snowflakes.

Chapter Twenty-Eight

Ghosted

When I told James I'd called a psychic and what she said, he confirmed that her assessment felt accurate to him. He said he was pretty good managing his emotions during the day. He stayed busy. He had a lot of distractions. But at night, when he got in bed alone, it all came flooding back.

We'd decided to put the brakes on any relationship. He said he just wasn't ready. That was a nice way to reframe all the chaos. I didn't argue. Friendship felt more sustainable. There was a lot more to him than I'd seen. I had so many questions, but they all felt too personal to ask. And I knew there wasn't anything I could say that would help.

We were both quiet and that felt like the right thing. It felt like the only thing but also, it felt good to just sit silently, taking it in together.

"She would have loved you," he said.

"I know she loved you! She loves you so much she's still trying to talk to you!"

"True," he laughed.

"I'll probably be like that." I confessed. "I have a hard time letting go. I'll be haunting everyone I know."

He laughed and I backtracked.

"I don't mean she's haunting you! She was so great in the dream. I mean, if that's a haunting I'm all for it! She can haunt me any time! Sorry."

"It's fine," he said. "She would think it was funny too. "You two would have been thick as thieves," he added.

I couldn't help but wonder what my life might have been like if I had met her when she was alive. Had we been destined to meet before her untimely death took that possibility away?

"Can I say something completely inappropriate but also funny?" I asked him.

"Of course," he said.

"It's really bad," I warned.

"Now you have to. That's my favorite," he encouraged.

"Okay," I said. "So, I've been thinking about how things are going with us. Dating is really hard."

"Right," he said. "I'm learning."

"And I've seen all the games people play, the breadcrumbing, slow fades, cheating, lies, ghosting."

I paused to make sure he was paying attention, then continued. "Dating you has really taken ghosting to the next level."

As I hoped, he burst out laughing, and I joined him until I snorted, tears rolling down my cheeks. I tried to apologize for snorting. It came out like a face fart. It always happened during the best laughs, but it made me sound like a donkey.

"I'm sorry!" I snorted again.

Now, James couldn't breathe either.

It's the worst thing. But even worse is if you got my family together, we all have it. The snorting is genetic!

"Thank you for that," James said when he finally caught his breath. His eyes were filled with tears. The good tears. "I really needed that."

Chapter Twenty-Nine

I Reject Your Curse

Dating was hard enough without all these extra layers. New emotions, experiences, the pandemic, stress, parenting, and now, another woman in the mix who happened to be dead. It was spring break. I'd made it through my Business Law class with a B. I had a week off before my next class started. Not only that, but I had a week off parenting and work too. My ex-husband was taking the kids to the UK for a week. James was also going to be traveling with his daughter. I would be home with my dog. Unsupervised.

For the first time in my adult life, I didn't have any major responsibilities. No kids, no school, no work. No nothing. My time was completely my own for one week.

In my mind, I was going to get everything on my list done and then still have time to relax and see friends. I felt hopeful. I was no longer on the verge of tears at any moment from any little stressor. I didn't feel like I was working on panic.

Other things were different, too. I started finding things that I had previously lost. In particular, I found a necklace that I loved and had searched for many times, emptying my jewelry boxes, rustling through drawers, and checking pockets. Then, all of a sudden, it was just sitting in one of the small square cups in my jewelry box. I couldn't explain it.

Thanks," I said out loud. "Can you drop a couple grand in there too?"

My financial situation was still dire and getting worse.

When my daughter started waitressing at sixteen, she needed transportation. My only car was a twelve-year-old minivan, which meant my son and I were stranded whenever she took it. Her dad and stepmom had three cars between them, but when I asked if she could use one during her weeks with me, he flatly refused.

I had no money but decent credit. In a move that would make financial advisors cringe, I traded my minivan for a used Mitsubishi Mirage, then immediately drove to another dealership and bought a Honda CRV for my daughter. By splitting the $20,000 debt between two dealers on the same day, the banks couldn't see the total burden I was taking on.

I had no clear plan for making the payments, but my daughter could work, and we both had transportation. I'd solved the immediate problem. I'd figure out the rest later. I always found a way. That was one thing I liked about me. No matter what it took, I always found a way. But now her car needed repairs, my credit cards were maxed, and I desperately needed money.

My first priority for spring break was to get Gunther to pay me for the website I'd built him. I hadn't heard from Gunther since sending him the files.

"Is everything okay with the website? Can you cut me that check?" I texted. Silence.

"Did you get my email?" I sent a couple hours later. Still nothing.

I looked online and noticed the website was up and running. It looked great. I saw he linked it to his LinkedIn profile and had shared the link on his page. Some of his vendors and customers had commented how nice it looked.

Finally, I heard his ding.

"You didn't do what I told you to do. There are errors all over the website. I'm going to have to redo it myself."

Immediately, the back of my neck felt hot, and my throat was closing in. I was shaking inside with anger.

I called Jae. "I literally used all the photos and text he gave me. The only things I changed were some spelling errors and the sizing and enhancements of some photos that were too dark."

"The website looks amazing," she said. "He's being an asshole. I knew he wouldn't pay."

I'd spent hours on that website when my time was already extremely limited. I'd created carousels of photos of his work. I'd created a map of job sites, just as he'd asked. When we started talking about the website years before he said he'd asked some professional developers to give him a quote and that page alone would have been thousands due to the programming.

I couldn't hold back my anger. I sent a scathing text to him. It was furious. It was hateful. It was filled with every ounce of anger I'd ever built up and suppressed toward him. It was fueled by the memory of three years of his betrayal, lies, and belittling comments. It was longer than a whole phone screen. It was a wall of text.

"Lol," he replied. Nothing else. Just "lol."

I felt like an idiot. He'd fooled me again. I trusted him again and wanted to think the best and he probably had no intentions of paying me to begin with. I hated him but more than that, I hated myself. I wanted to hurt him. I wanted to say something so hurtful that it would sting. I wanted to say the meanest thing I could think of so that he would feel even remotely as terrible as I was feeling.

At the same time, I was afraid to be mean. I knew that whatever mean thing I said, he would come back with something a thousand times meaner, and I would not be able to handle it. I also didn't want to say anything evil. I wanted it to sting but I didn't want to be cruel, I just wanted my pain to be known. I wanted my pain to be seen.

I typed and erased my message several times then finally landed on what I felt would express my anger without being evil. I wasn't wishing any permanent harm and yet, it was awful.

"I hope you shit your pants and have to sit in it." Send.

Almost immediately he replied. I was afraid to look at it. I braced myself knowing he could devastate me with a single word.

"I reject your curse," he wrote.

That was a strange thing to say. I'd never heard him talk like that. It stunned me out of my anger and into a mix of confusion and reflection. What would that even do? I felt ashamed that I'd sent it. It wasn't satisfying. It didn't make me feel any better. Even if it had hurt him, I knew it wouldn't have made me feel better. I wanted my own pain to stop.

That night, Monday, March 5th, I had plans to meet my friend Adrienne for dinner. I hadn't seen her in a year, but she insisted we go out to eat and catch up. She lived in town, so we met in the middle at a little Tex-Mex restaurant about twenty minutes away. I didn't get to see friends often because I was always too busy or didn't want to spend money, but it was spring break, and I'd worked hard at school and knew I deserved to celebrate making it through another class.

It felt so good to spend time with her and catch up. It reminded me that there really are people who love me, who like me and who want to spend time with me for me. I felt the same way about her and silently vowed in my mind to be a better friend. I didn't tell her about what had happened with Gunther. The whole situation was so emotional and strange. I didn't know what to make of it and was embarrassed by how I'd acted.

Toward the end of dinner, I felt my stomach rumbling. It wasn't a hunger pang. It felt more like gas. I couldn't recall eating anything earlier that day that would upset my stomach. We were having a great time talking and I didn't want to cut it short, but my stomach was quickly feeling more and more unsettled.

I told her I'd have to get home to let the dog out and flagged down the waitress for the check. I just wanted to be home. My stomach was turning in knots. We paid and walked out front. I gave her a hurried hug and went to my car.

I hadn't been in my car longer than an instant when it happened. I shit my pants, or more accurately, my dress. I had no control over it. I didn't push. It just slipped out like a greased potato, fully formed and solid, but it immediately smashed into mashed potatoes when I shifted my weight in horror. Is this really my life? Did I just shit myself?

Adrienne drove by and waved.

What do I even do in this situation? Do I throw it away? But then I'd have to touch it. It wasn't loose or liquid which added to the confusion as to how it even happened.

I pulled into a dark parking spot behind a Wendy's and tried to figure out what to do. I carefully slid my underwear off with the bundle of poo inside it and wrapped it in the long fabric of my skirt which I had pulled to the side of my thigh to use as a pouch while I drove. I was afraid it would fall out next to my leg and roll under the seat with all the coins and crumbs. I drove home in shock holding a hot shit in the fabric of my dress, feeling it slowly cool. There were so many other cars on the road. Nice people driving places, not holding a potato sized shit in their hand like me.

When I got home, I carefully exited the car, walked to the side of my driveway next to the fence and dumped it into the yard. I went fully clothed into the shower, rinsing the rest of the dung off my dress and myself.

I reject your curse! Gunther's retort volleyed from one side of my brain to the other. Did my mean words bounce off him like rubber and stick to me like glue? Was that real too? First ghosts, now this? What on earth was going on?

Chapter Thirty

The Urging

I decided it was safer to stay home the next few days and not talk to anyone. Were my words that powerful? Had I cast a spell? I was completely healthy after the incident. There was nothing to suggest I had a stomach bug. Clearly, I had sent a powerful bad intention into the world, Gunther had rejected it and I'd gotten the full force of it. I froze at what could have happened if I hadn't pumped the brakes before lashing out. And I wondered if sending out powerful good thoughts would also bring good things back to me.

"I hope everyone has a good day!" I said out loud.

Almost immediately, Gunther texted, "I have a check for you, I can drop it off tomorrow."

"I thought you didn't like the website." I texted back flatly.

"I'm sorry. I was mad," he replied.

"Ok, thank you," I replied, uncertain if I could count on it.

After almost thirty minutes, he texted again, "I love you."

Tears welled up in my eyes, blinding me immediately, "I know," I replied, "I love you too." I did love him. I just didn't love the confusion. He was one of my favorite people, when things were good. And my least favorite when things were bad. I wished they could just be good, all the time but I was coming to terms with the fact that I just needed to appreciate the good times and let go of any expectation it would be different.

Our love was buried under hot, unrestrained passions and raw unhealed wounds. This was the pattern. Passion then peace. Neither of us knew how to handle it. The only thing to do was go our separate ways and do no harm.

My mind was racing, so I decided to get to work on all my projects.

Part of me believed that if I could just organize my house, get caught up on chores, everything else would fall into place and my life would be fixed.

The first thing I did was clean those coops out. I raked all the bedding into my rusty wheelbarrow then dumped the clippings in the back of my property where the chickens would spread it around until it become dirt. I hosed down and dried the coops then sprayed with apple cider vinegar then when it dried, I put in new bedding. It was dusty, dirty, sweaty, physical work, but it felt good to be in the fresh air, using my body to improve things. Anything was better than sitting in my desk chair staring at a computer screen trying to meet artificially urgent deadlines.

As I worked, my mind drifted. I wondered how my kids were enjoying Europe with their father. I imagined the cold, the hustle and bustle of a big city, the accents. I wondered how my coworkers were faring with all the deadlines while there was one less person to carry the workload. Then, my thoughts drifted to James on his trip with his daughter. I wondered if we would keep talking to each other when he got back.

Things had gotten quite strange, first the dream, and then me running out of his house crying. We'd scaled back to friendship, but this week apart would be a great opportunity for things to slowly fade away into no contact at all.

As I thought about James, an overwhelming sensation started to take over. It was a strong yearning, almost urgent, as if I needed to reach out to him. It made no sense. I had decided to give him space, even resigning myself to the idea that he might ghost me. Why was I missing him? And why this sudden, inexplicable urge to say I loved him?

I think she's trying to tell me something, he'd said the day I told him about the dream. Could this be her? Did visitation dreams happen while awake as well?

All I knew was these thoughts, these feelings, none of them were mine, yet they seemed to be running parallel to my own. It was like two voices in my head, mine and hers, overlapping and intertwining until I couldn't tell where I ended, and she began.

It was unsettling and, frankly, terrifying. For all the times I'd wished I didn't have to live this life anymore, I felt intensely possessive over my own body and my own life. It wasn't the life I wanted but I wasn't going to just hand it over to some dead woman either. It was my life. I wanted to keep it.

Maybe if I just told James her message, it would be enough, and she would leave me alone.

The relationship felt doomed already. Between the dream and my breakdown, this would surely put a fork in it. If the relationship couldn't be saved, maybe at least my sanity could be. I would just send him all these thoughts; she'd get her message across and then she could leave me alone.

"Hear me out," I texted. "I feel like I need to tell you something. I know it's weird, but it feels important, and it doesn't feel like it's coming from me. If it doesn't make sense, just ignore it. We'll pretend this never happened."

"Sure," he replied.

I stared at my phone, took a deep breath, and started typing. It felt as though I was both a participant and an observer in my own mind, caught between two worlds. As I typed, an image of James and his daughter flashed vividly in my mind. I saw them driving through a mountain pass, his daughter's feet on the dash as she scrolled through her phone. James was focused on the road, loud music blaring from the radio. It was so clear, it felt like I was there with them.

My finger hovered over the send button, and a rush of adrenaline coursed through me. There's no coming back from this, I thought, bracing myself for what came next. This is definitely super weird. Then, with one quick motion, I hit send.

"I love you so much," the message said, though I didn't love him. "I'm so proud of you, and I'm grateful for everything you're doing for our daughter."

"That's not me," I followed up with, in case there was any confusion.

The moment I pressed send, a wave of calm washed over me. The urge had disappeared. I felt ridiculous, but the anxiety was gone. I hoped that was the last of it.

I went back to my chores, feeling strangely relieved. About thirty minutes later, I got a text from James.

"Hey, sorry for the delay. We're on the interstate, driving through the Tennessee mountains. Just stopped for gas."

The image of them driving replayed in my mind, crystal clear. A shiver ran through me. This wasn't a coincidence. This was real, undeniably real.

I watched the three dots appear and disappear on my phone as James typed. My heart pounded. Finally, his message came through.

"I want to tell her about you," he wrote, referring to his daughter. "I want to tell her that her mother is communicating through you and that her mother is okay. We could feel Julie in the car. We were listening to her playlist, and both of us felt her." He was describing it just as I saw it earlier.

He continued, "I spoke to a medium about you. I told her about your dream. She suggested that you might be spiritually open, so she's able to communicate through you. What do you think? Should I tell my daughter about you?"

Telling his daughter about me opened up cans of worms. He'd kept it a secret that he met me and was seeing me. I was racing out of the house not only for his privacy but for her protection. While he wanted female company and physical comfort, his daughter would have been hurt by the perception her father was moving on while they were both still grieving.

It was too big a question for me. I didn't want the responsibility of answering it.

"I don't think I can answer that." I replied, feeling the uncertainty sink in.

I set my phone down and walked away, trying to clear my head. I walked from my bedroom to the kitchen, past the couch. Before I even made it to the back door to go look at the chickens, I had an answer. Except—it wasn't my answer. It was Julie's. *She* knew.

I rushed back to my phone.

"Don't tell her," I texted. "I'm not here for her. I'm here for you. She's going to have a dream, just like the one I had. She'll be able to communicate with her mom on her own."

"Okay," he replied.

A few days later, while unloading groceries from their crinkly thin bags into my fridge, I got another text from James.

"She had a dream about her mother last night," James wrote. "She woke up happy. The dream was detailed, just like yours. Her whole demeanor has changed. She's talkative and laughing. She says it felt like her mom was right there with her. You were right. Thank you."

I stared at the message, my heart both heavy and light, a strange combination of awe and relief settling over me. Somehow, I had been the bridge between two worlds, and this connection had helped his daughter who was suffering. I was in awe of what happened and the part I had played in it. As embarrassing as it felt at the time, sending the text had given James information that helped his daughter come out of despair, even just a little. Having Julie communicate through me didn't feel scary anymore, it felt sacred. She had used me to help. That made me feel special and valuable in a way I'd never felt before.

Chapter Thirty-One

The Presence

Still filled with awe and gratitude, I went to the living room to tackle a basket of laundry. As I folded the clothes, I reflected on his daughter's dream, and my dream. Julie had shown up in dreams, and somehow, she had also appeared when I was awake. Yet, this time, I wasn't just an observer; I was woven into the experience.

But why? Was it just my connection to her husband? Or was it like James had said, that I was more spiritually open and that made me the right person to help her deliver her message?

I reflected on how it felt when I was aware of that urging presence within me. It felt like the part of me that holds my thoughts and opinions shifted to the left inside my body, making space as she squeezed in on the right. It was like someone squeezing a chair in beside you at a table when there is already not enough space. I moved over instinctively, out of courtesy, not realizing that when I shifted, she would have the better seat at the table.

I was seeing this was a theme in my life. I was accommodating to others, even to the point of neglecting myself. But this time, instead of pushing me out of the way completely without any consideration of my needs, she also brought me a sense of peace, she included me, and I felt like I was part of something special.

Could it be that my kindness and openness, traits that had so often left me exposed and wounded were, in fact key to this process? Could it be that the very qualities that once invited harm were the very ones that allowed me to respond to her nudges?

I carried the folded laundry to my son's room, placing the organized piles on his bed. Then I went to the dryer and unloaded another basketful of warm clothes and returned to the couch to continue folding.

As I folded, my movements became automatic, the repetitive rhythm of sorting, matching and folding lulled me into something deeper, a state I didn't recognize. But soon, it felt less like I was folding clothes and more like I was floating.

It's one thing to have a dream so vivid it feels real, but it's something else entirely when reality itself starts to feel like a dream.

In this dreamy state, I became aware of someone beside me on the couch and others in my living room. There was a man sitting to my right, a woman across from me in a chair, and a third being, neither male nor female, floating near the ceiling. Though invisible, their presence was palpable, as if the space they were taking up was buzzing and flickering.

As the man next to me communicated, my perception of the world transformed. Everything that had been solid now felt wispy, like tissue paper, including me. My vision was neither close nor far. The air shimmered. It was as if the fabric of reality itself, the pieces that held everything together, were gently coming into focus, like emerging from under water.

I was aware of everything in every direction. Not only in three hundred and sixty degrees around me but also into the cosmos and thousands of years ahead and thousands of years into the past. My body buzzed, not with dizziness but with fizz. I felt effervescent.

Chapter Thirty-Two

The Promise

As he sat beside me, he began explaining my life to me as if he were telling me a well-known story. His explanations were both compassionate and matter of fact. And as he spoke, I didn't just hear the words—I understood them at a level far deeper than thought. He showed me the connections I have with others, explaining that some bonds are stronger than others. When he described them, I saw the bonds as a line that lit up as he spoke. These lines were between me and everyone I knew. They were also between me and places, events, and ideas.

As he spoke, I felt an overwhelming sense of relief. The things I had agonized over for years, the endless ruminations and doubts. They suddenly lost their heaviness. I saw them from a neutral perspective, without blame, shame, guilt or fear. The events in my life just "were what they were."

He shared truths I hadn't even thought to wonder about, yet they made immediate sense, as though they were always there, waiting for me to recognize them. It was so much information, far more than I could process all at once, yet he delivered it with ease, as if passing me a note. It should have been overwhelming—too much, too fast. But instead, it felt easy. It was so easy I didn't question any of it, not the man speaking to me, not the sparkling room, not the figure floating at my ceiling. Even the surreal nature of it all seemed perfectly natural in that moment.

Here are some of the things he told me.

The baby I miscarried was actually my son. The same son I later gave birth to after my daughter. My children had chosen to be mine together. When the first opportunity to incarnate arose, my son was ready and waiting. His sister was off socializing. When she realized she'd missed the chance, she asked him to let her go first. She wanted to be the older sister. As is his nature, he agreed. I miscarried, then soon got pregnant again. She came first, and he followed two years after her.

I have strong energy that has the power to attract and repel equally. Because many live only in logic, when their hearts want to lead, fear takes over. They don't run from me; they run from themselves.

Love isn't out of reach; it just looks different.

What feels like rejection is either preparation for something better or protection from something worse.

Follow the nudges. Life is constantly guiding me through intuitive nudges. This is my spiritual compass. Resistance to the nudges creates suffering. The pain isn't punishment, it's communication.

Everything I need already exists within me or around me. I lack nothing. I have so many resources.

The universe responds to clear requests. Ask specifically for what I need.

Doubt is a powerful and destructive force that creates a gulf between me and what was meant for me. Reject it.

Failure is not real. The concept of failure is an illusion.

Failed relationship weren't rejections of me, they were rejecting themselves.

I wanted to know why my life had so many challenges despite having so many privileges and opportunities. In therapy, over the years, the therapists always searched for childhood trauma to explain my pattern of abusive relationships and low self-worth. But I had loving parents and a wonderful childhood. It didn't make sense. They sometimes accused me of not remembering. But I knew. I just didn't fit the textbook.

"You have to look at all the lifetimes, not just this one," he said.

"There's more?"

They flashed in front of me. He didn't just answer my questions; he also gave me all of the context and capacity to understand the answers deeply. In an instant.

Then, with a strength of mind that transferred to me so strongly I felt it take root in me, he said, "You are the only one who has ever doubted you. No one, no one, anywhere, at any time, in any lifetime, galaxy, or beyond has ever doubted you."

Then, one last question rose up: "Why now?"

"You asked."

I saw a flash of myself at my kitchen table, with the sewing machine in front of me during Covid. I was sewing masks. I was feeding fabric under the foot and watching the needle punch holes of thread in a straight line lit up by the tiny light on the belly of the machine and I could hear my own thoughts, the thoughts I was having in that moment.

"If I've got to be here, God, just use me for something good," I prayed in my mind. I was oblivious to what began to stir around me.

But it wasn't just this one instance of me asking to serve. I was able to see a multitude of scenes where my heart was volunteering to do something brave, in this and other lifetimes.

I watched these scenes with new eyes. I watched myself as an observer. I saw myself like I was looking at someone else. This woman was creative, confident and courageous. She had a beautiful, generous heart that was open and hopeful. She was genuine and honest. She was lovable and loved. She had the ability to bring out the best in others, to help them believe in themselves in new ways.

While I had been consumed with my own suffering, there was a bigger story happening in my life without me knowing it. This story was more expansive. It was about resilience, courage and being an inspiration to others. This story was so moving I found myself overwhelmed with deep admiration for this woman who was me. I would have done anything to get to know a woman like her, even briefly. But I didn't need to meet her, I *was* her. I was seeing myself through their eyes.

"You could have done it sooner though!" The woman's voice interjected. She wasn't talking to me; she was talking to him.

The man beside me chuckled, and even the energy hovering above us seemed humored. Then, they started talking amongst themselves, and I could hear them.

"Can you imagine?" The one hovering mused and showed a quick moving image of me if things had gone differently.

I couldn't really see what was so different, but they could.

"It would have been fine to tell her sooner!" she insisted.

"She's got no brakes!" the presence near the ceiling said.

"That's a good thing!" the woman insisted.

"You see," the man next to me explained, "You make a big ripple. You have impact that you don't even see. You needed to build resilience. Your waves crash into other waves. This is good, even necessary, but you needed preparation to stay strong in the storms. And your kids? They just needed you to be their mom. They needed you to simply be present."

They had allowed me to do things my way for long enough, but I had gone so far off my path, they had to intervene. I was so far off track that I wasn't going to find my way back without their help.

My entire life suddenly made sense on a level that was beyond any I'd ever considered. Everything they conveyed felt true beyond argument. I saw myself as awe inspiring beyond description, magical, even mind blowing. I saw myself as incredibly thoughtful, kind and loving. I was completely selfless. I couldn't argue with what I saw. I knew it to be true. Not only that, but I could see the people around me in that same incredible light. My kids, Jae, Gunther, friends, my parents, my ex-husband...anyone I thought of flashed into my mind and I saw them for who they truly were. They were amazing, talented, genius, brave. I saw their pain too. Their own self-doubt, their own fears. They were afraid, uncertain, hopeful, overwhelmed. I saw them through God's eyes not just how they appeared to me in the narrow lens of my own personal experience.

I felt so overwhelmed with love for everything and everyone, including myself. I felt my heart expanding and as if my body was lifting to the ceiling by the lightness of my heart. I was laughing, deliriously.

The man beside me got up to leave and as he was standing, he reached into my energy in the space around me and grabbed things as if he were plucking them off a table. "I'm going to take these too," he said, grabbing more things that had been scattered around my energy. They were blocks I hadn't even noticed until he began to remove them. He took my shame over mistakes I made. He took guilt over things I had or hadn't said. He took judgments I had toward myself and others. He took blocks that were covering insights. He was tidying up, removing beliefs and that had no purpose. He was removing anxiety, fear and self-doubt like they were objects scattered in my energetic field. He put them in a gigantic bag to haul them away.

"You don't need these," he said.

When they were gone, I still felt as if I was floating, lighter than air. I felt bubbly and full of giggles. I couldn't stop laughing. I didn't question what had happened. I didn't wonder what else he had taken with him. I didn't analyze the experience at all, I simply soaked it up. I felt completely safe, at peace, and filled with love and comfort and overwhelming joy. Everything was more than okay. It was amazing.

After a short while, I noticed the laundry basket filled with folded clothes and carried it back to my daughter's room. Everything felt surreal. As I put the clothes away, I giggled and giggled. The giggling was like Julie's giggle in the dream. It was constant and sustaining almost like breathing.

Slowly, though, an awareness began to creep in. The experience began to fade and as I began to reorient myself with my familiar reality, I felt a rising panic. I hadn't questioned the presence, the messages, the feeling of being out of body, or the elation when it was happening. But once it was over, gravity returned and so did the heavy feelings.

I knew that what had happened was extraordinary. I didn't know what to make of it. I found a notebook to write it all down in as much detail as I could remember. At the top of the page, I printed the date. March 7, 2023. It was less than a month since the dream. Nearly two months since I met James. And while I hoped it was the last of the unbelievable experiences, it was still the very beginning.

Chapter Thirty-Three

It's My Cousin's Fault

The next few days were strange. When I tried to replay the incident, instead of it being like a typical memory, fuzzy around the edges with only the highlights remaining, it was like I could revisit it. I could simply think about what it felt like and parts of it would be repeated but even more expansive. More questions answered.

I stared at my couch. Was it really a couch? What was real?

Clearly, I'd had a psychotic break. There was no other explanation. Logically, I knew this was alarming, but I felt so unbothered and at peace. I tried to get anxious. I tried to get my shoulders tight and to dig into the panic of "Oh my God I'm a lunatic!" But it didn't work. I felt neutral. When the man grabbed things from my energy, he took my anxiety. I couldn't even fake it. It was like I was play acting. I tried again to freak out. I tried to get my heart racing, I lifted my eyebrows and inhaled sharply, "Oh no! I've lost my mind!" But it was comical. I couldn't do it. He'd taken all my senseless worries. He'd taken all my unnecessary fucks. There was nothing to worry about. Everything was going to be okay. Everything was going to be great.

I read through my notes trying to make sense of it all, I suddenly remembered something my cousin had said the night before the visitation dream. She said she was going to write something in her manifestation journal.

I called her immediately.

"Do you remember when I went to the hockey game with James?"

"Yes? Are you okay?"

"Yes, but I think all this is because of you."

"Me?"

"Yes, remember you said you were going to try to manifest something for me? What was it? What did you write?"

"I don't remember, I'll have to look."

"When you find it, please send it to me."

"Okay, I will. I'll be home in about an hour."

I wasn't sure why I suddenly remembered that but once it was in my mind I couldn't forget it.

About an hour later she texted me. I took a screen shot with the date so I could remember it forever.

It said: "Kathryn- to find peace in her heart and soul to be her own source of fulfillment. To love and accept herself unconditionally. To embrace "anything is possible." Dream Big.

I definitely was feeling peace in my heart. I felt content and protected. I felt loved and I had a greater understanding of myself that made me really like myself. It all mattered. It all had a purpose. There was nothing wrong with me, in fact I was sort of impressed. I was pretty special.

Chapter Thirty-Four

Psychological Evaluation

I moved my therapy appointment up a week. I needed a professional opinion. I was so used to the floor dropping out from under me that it was hard to believe this feeling of elation would last and not be followed by something awful. I had to make a plan for the eventual collapse.

"Something strange has happened," I began. "I think it might be bad."

I had insisted we meet on zoom. I wasn't sure if she was going to haul me away and have me committed.

"Is everyone okay?" she asked quickly. "Your kids, you?"

"We're all fine. It's me. I think the stress finally got to me. I've had a breakdown. I don't feel like myself."

"Tell me more." Natalie was prepared with her notebook.

"It started with that dream I told you about, but that wasn't the end of it. Strange things are still happening. I'm hearing things. I'm hearing voices. I think I'm schizophrenic."

"That does sound unsettling," she said calmly. She wrote something down. "But let's not jump to conclusions."

She asked about the usual topics: work, kids, school. I wanted to get back to the voices. She was getting off topic. She didn't seem to understand the severity, but I didn't know how much to share. Should I mention the curse that bounced back like rubber and stuck to me like glue? Should I tell her about feeling like Julie was in my body making me text James? What about sitting on my couch talking to people who weren't there? The fits of giggles? I didn't want her to institutionalize me, I just wanted a game plan. I needed to present my mental breakdown in an approachable way so we could make a pragmatic plan to tackle it so that it wouldn't interfere with my responsibilities.

"Is there a test for schizophrenia you can give me?" I asked.

"You're not schizophrenic," she said, gently but firmly. "This doesn't match the clinical picture for schizophrenia."

"But I'm hearing things. I'm hallucinating? Doesn't that ...?"

She interrupted me, "What kinds of things are you hearing?

"More like...I'm feeling voices. I feel them somewhere around here." I pointed to my neck, almost behind my ear.

"And what are you hearing? Is it cruel or harmful?"

"No. They're uh ... encouraging. They tell me I'm loved. They tell me I should believe in myself."

She smiled. "That's good."

I blinked.

"I know this feels strange," she continued, "but this doesn't fit any clinical diagnosis. At the very least we would have to track this to see patterns over time. Schizophrenia is complex. It includes loss of reality, disorganized thinking, and dysfunction. You're functioning very well. You just described your experience in a coherent, even engaging, way."

I could see her point, but I wasn't convinced.

"I don't want to dismiss your feelings," she continued. "But let's look at this differently. You're less anxious, your sleeping patterns are improved, you are saying encouraging things to yourself, you're developing a positive outlook, releasing negative thought patterns—this is exactly the outcome we were working toward, right? This is the goal of therapy. The fact that it came suddenly, well, maybe you were just ready."

"The voices though?" I asked.

"Maybe you've always had a running narrative in your head and now it's just switched to a better script," she said.

The session was nearly over. I didn't want the session to end. I wanted to hear her explain this more.

"There are a lot of ways to move through the world," she continued. "There's a lot of room for a variety of experiences. Just because something is unusual or unconventional doesn't mean we need to pathologize it. The transformation you are experiencing is something every single one of my clients is wanting to experience. Every single one of my friends, too. The fact that it was fast and unexpected doesn't diminish the positive outcomes."

What she was telling me resonated. The experience overall felt positive. I did feel much better. It just sounded so crazy the way it happened.

"Kathryn, does it really matter how we get there? I've counseled hundreds of people and healing looks different for everyone. You are on a positive path, keep going. I think if you give yourself some time to process this you will feel better. Write it down. I know you like to write. Writing your experience might help others going through something similar someday. Keep an open mind."

"Okay," I agreed.

"Maybe pick up some books on spiritual awakenings," she said almost as an afterthought. "This might not be that unusual after all. Spiritual awakenings often seem otherworldly, but they've been happening since the beginning of time.

"Thank you," I said with genuine gratitude. "See you soon."

She wasn't wrong. I still had that deep sense that everything would be okay. I couldn't explain it, but I could feel it.

Chapter Thirty-Five

The Kundalini

"She said I'm not crazy," I told my cousin over the phone.

"I never thought you were crazy," she replied.

"I love that about you," I said. "She said it's pretty common. She said it might be a spiritual awakening. I've been googling it. Apparently, people try to have this happen to them."

"A kundalini awakening," she said.

"A kunda-what?" I asked.

"It happens to yogis. They meditate for years, and eventually, this electric energy, like a snake, travels up their spine from their butt and they become better people, full of love and endless patience."

"Sounds nice... except for the snake in the butt thing," I said.

"Joe Rogan talks about it," she added.

"I knew Joe Rogan was into butt stuff!"

"He and Jordan Peterson talked about using meditation to achieve psychadelic states of mind."

This was getting even more bizarre, "Joe Rogan and Jordan Peterson had spiritual awakenings?"

"I don't think so," she explained. "They just do the drugs and yoga to try. All the cold-plunge bros are microdosing psilocybin now."

"Psilo-what?"

"Magic mushrooms."

"Ohh!"

"Spirituality is their new competition."

"Great," I replied. "The cold plunge bros ruin everything."

I looked up Kundalini awakenings. I hadn't felt a fiery surge of energy going up my spine. I hadn't been meditating. I wasn't on a journey. I wasn't seeking. I was struggling. I was matching socks.

Chapter Thirty-Six

I'm Rubber, You're Glue

The memory of falling into that pit of despair in James's bed didn't just haunt me, it terrified me. One moment I was myself, the next I was drowning in someone else's emotional undertow. I felt hopeless and afraid. I wanted out. Everything I had worked with Natalie to recover from came crashing back in an instant and it took days to find my way back to the surface. If this could happen during a simple nap, what else would send me into a freefall, and when? I didn't want to feel like that ever again.

Monica had said I needed to protect my energy, but what even *was* my energy? And how, exactly, was I supposed to protect it?

Before all this, "energy" just meant stamina: morning energy, evening fatigue, the mid-afternoon slump. It was something you lost with effort and restored with food, rest, or caffeine. But now, suddenly *everything* was energy. And somehow, that made the concept less helpful, not more.

I quickly grew frustrated by the advice:

"Raise your vibration!"

"Your frequency is too low!"

"Resonate with joy!"

What the hell was everyone talking about? I had no idea. It was so foreign to my experience it offended me. It was like when I was juggling two toddlers, a job, cooking, cleaning, activities and bills and someone would say, "Just take a break."

"No Asshole! Come help me then! Don't just tell me where to dig, pick up a shovel so I can take a break! It's just me!" It enraged me like they were saying, just stop caring for one of your kids if it's too much. I didn't have a choice. I had to do everything I was doing. It was only me doing everything, couldn't they see that!?

It was insulting. It suggested the lack of results came from a lack of effort or intelligence when really, it was just way too much for anyone!

Because, seriously, how do you "tap into gratitude" when you're living in fear? How do you "manifest your highest timeline" when you feel like you're drowning?

"Raise Your Vibration" was the equivalent of Marie Antoinette standing from her balcony of privilege shouting down to all the plebes like me saying, "Let them eat Light!"

How am I supposed to be spiritual when I don't even know what people are talking about? What was Julie thinking coming to me for spiritual support? I was the least likely candidate.

I was a fireball of emotion: reactive, impatient, quick to anger. Being spiritual was supposed to make me loving and peaceful. Instead, it was making me angry and fiery. I had no namaste; I was full of No-Mas-Today!"

Despite my resistance, I decided to try meditating. I had nothing to lose.

Chapter Thirty-Seven

Learning to Meditate

As frustrating as it was, I needed to start somewhere. I started with guided meditations that taught me to focus on my breath. What did it feel like to breathe? How did my chest expand or contract? Was the air cool or warm? What did my heart feel like? Did it pound or flutter? What was my body doing? Was I comfortable? Were my muscles tight or relaxed? This taught me to recognize what it felt like to be me, physically. Even being hungry or needing to use the bathroom were relevant data points. I studied myself. What made my body feel different on Tuesday than it did on Sunday? Was any of that in my control?

Next, we moved to my mind. This was harder but I got the hang of it. What were my thoughts? What thoughts were unpleasant, what were supportive? What thoughts led to other thoughts? And what thoughts led to a sense of completion?

I determined that "me" was the state where I felt good and at ease in my mind and my body. I was alert but calm. Everything that wasn't alert and calm was "not me." Feeling distracted, agitated, under pressure, worried, these were states that came outside of me.

Protecting my peace became more tactical when I understood that my peace was a state of being I could control. Just as Gunther had instantly rejected my curse, I needed to instantly reject anything that threatened my calm center.

The irony wasn't lost on me: for years, I'd been working myself to exhaustion, pushing harder, doing more, always with the underlying belief that I needed to earn my place, earn love, earn security. I'd created a life where worth was measured in output and sacrifice, never in simply being. I thought peace was passive and unproductive. I thought action and effort got results and when I didn't get results, I thought I was doing it wrong, wasn't working hard enough. I doubled down on hustle.

Now here I was, being asked to protect something I'd never believed was inherently valuable: me, just as I am.

Chapter Thirty-Eight

Expanded Vision

O dd things were happening around me. Nothing quite as dramatic as the experience on the couch or even the dream, but things were notably different from before. For starters, I was able to see auras on some people. On some, it looked like a soft backlight, on others an outline, and on others their aura looked pillowy as if it had texture and substance.

The first aura I'd seen on someone else was my dad's. I was visiting for a weekend. We were in my childhood home. He was standing in the doorway between the kitchen and dining room, telling me a story. He was animated. I can't even remember what he was talking about because at some point, I stopped listening and was just watching a halo of aqua light surrounding him. It was radiating out of him, moving and shifting. It was animated, just like he was.

I was seeing him not just as my dad but with the same vision I had on the couch. I saw him for who he truly was outside of just my knowledge of him. I saw how kind and giving he was. I saw all the ways he'd helped people in his life, not just me but others in the family, my brother, my mother, even people I'd never met. I was seeing his whole story in that glowing aqua color.

Then, I started to see light and color not just around people but between them, connecting everything to everything else. I saw myself as a pin on a board, with everyone around me as neighboring pins, connected by threads of colored light. Everyone had multiple threads attached to them, connecting them to other people, places, and ideas. The threads were all different colors, textures, and thicknesses, and the pins moved, like dancers around a maypole.

A week after that, when I was drifting to sleep, I saw a woman standing next to my bed. She had curly brown hair pulled up in loose buns on either side of her head. She wore red acrylic eyeglasses. She looked mid-forties. I had no idea who she was. Just as quickly as she appeared, she was gone.

Then a few weeks later, it happened again. This time it was a man in a business suit. He came up to me, kneeled to tie his shoe, then vanished.

Who were these people? What was happening? Am I losing it?

I answered myself with a laugh, "No, you're getting it!"

I loved my new inner dialogue. I had this new cheerleader voice inside my head that kept encouraging me. Was it Julie? Was it me? Did it matter?

The faces themselves didn't scare me. They startled me, but I felt they were trying to tell me something or they needed me. I felt bad that I didn't know how to help them. Who were they? And what did they want?

I needed someone who understood what was happening. I needed a psychic medium. I found a metaphysical store in Wilmington. I booked a session with a kind-looking psychic, spending money I didn't have because this felt urgent.

The store was called Alchemy & Aura. It was tucked between a bakery and a Thai grocery, filled with crystals, books, and perfumed with incense. We went back to her private room for the reading.

"So, I had a spiritual awakening," I blurted. "I was folding laundry when people who weren't really there talked to me. Before that, a dead woman I had never known visited me in my dream. I was sleeping with her husband—but I mean, they weren't together anymore because, obviously, she was dead."

She shuffled her cards and asked me to cut the deck.

"Let me start again. I've been seeing faces, and a friend suggested I might be a medium. I don't know if the faces are dead people, and if they are, am I supposed to do something? They don't ever say anything. They just look at me and then disappear."

She listened patiently as I rambled, then asked, "Can you ask your guides?"

"I don't have a guide. I'm looking for a guide. Can you be my guide?" I asked.

"Your spirit guides," she explained gently.

"Yes, I'd like to have a spirit guide. Are you available?" I didn't want to spend more money, but maybe this is how it worked.

"You already have spirit guides, they've been with you since birth," she continued. "Those faces might be spirits trying to communicate or they might be your guide."

She instructed me to meditate each morning and ask them to reveal themselves. "Notice patterns, animals that appear repeatedly, songs that come on at just the right moment. There are meditations you can listen to that will help you communicate with them."

"Guided meditations?" I asked. "I've already been listening to some, I like them."

"Yes," she replied. "I can recommend a few or you can just search for them and use what resonates."

I was getting more questions than answers but starting to find my way around. No one was dismissing my experience. She was so friendly and receptive. I bought a couple crystals and a deck of cards before I left. I wasn't sure what I would do with them, but they were pretty and seemed to be staples of the trade.

Chapter Thirty-Nine

Mr. Messy

I was meditating more with the app. As soon as I tried to quiet my mind it filled with lists: grocery lists, to-do lists, packing lists but the guided meditations gave me something to think about, so I didn't think my own thoughts. But eventually, the narration started to distract me. I would feel myself moving into a deeper state of relaxation, and then the voice would come back and startle me or make me lose track of what I was experiencing.

So, I started to just listen to music or landscape sounds like waterfalls. With my eyes closed, I would first see static, like the white noise on a TV screen without a signal. Then it would blend it into a flat screen of grey, then I would make my body feel the same way until I felt like I was both inside vastness and was vastness itself. I called this "the soup."

When I was in the soup, a purple line of scribble would appear in my left periphery. It looked like Mr. Messy from the children's books. Sometimes it would approach me, sometimes its lines would melt, and the indigo color would wash over the grey soup. This scribble appeared almost every time I meditated deeply.

I'd looked up spirit guides and heard channelers talk about Archangel Michael, Native American tribe leaders, or even aliens from other galaxies as their guides. Suzanne Giesemann has a whole team of spirits called Sanaya. Was this scribble my spirit guide?

Finally, I decided it didn't matter if it was Mr. Messy answering me. I had a guide, at least I was claiming him as my guide. If he didn't like it, he'd have to speak up. I was sick of searching. If my guide was a purple scribble so be it.

Chapter Forty

Accessing Expanded Wisdom

Meditation wasn't just giving me a way to connect with my own energy, it was also giving me a way to retreat into a receptive state where information could enter without the constant filtering of my analytical mind. I remembered the man on the couch telling me that the universe responded to clear requests. So, I started to ask direct questions.

At first, I was frustrated that the answers didn't come immediately like they had on the couch, but they did come eventually. Most often, it would come a day or two later, when I'd already forgotten all about it. I would be doing something mindless like washing dishes, feeding the chickens, or driving, I'd suddenly get a massive insight, or something would pop into focus giving me clarity.

Was it Mr. Messy answering me? Was it Julie? Was it me? I knew this was related to meditating. Meditating created a receptive space. Meditation was the invitation. It was a container inside my hectic, overscheduled day where insights would drop in. It would take time to digest them. They would arrive in the meditation, but I wouldn't understand it until later.

The information I received was always bigger and broader than the question I asked. It didn't look like what I expected, but it was exactly what I needed at the time. The other interesting thing was that the information always came wrapped in a feeling. It brought with it peace and a sense of comfort. Often, I noticed a physical comfort as well. My body felt soft and tingly, and any pain or achiness I was experiencing would vanish.

Chapter Forty-One

Oneness Isn't Sameness

O ne day, while waiting at a stoplight, my senses stretched wide open. My forehead buzzed like it was made of cotton candy and I slipped into that same expanded state I'd felt on the couch. Cars whooshed past in rhythmic pulses, each one drawing me deeper into stillness.

And then it hit me: we are all the same, and yet entirely ourselves. One light, refracted through infinite lives.

There I go, I thought, as a car passed. There I go again, living out another story. I could feel myself in everyone: in the truck driver with a family, in the woman beside me with eyes full of fatigue. Every face, every car, every heartbeat, I knew them all because they were all some version of me.

I'd been wrestling with the idea of *oneness*. It came up constantly in books, podcasts, spiritual circles, but it always left me uneasy. It sounded like sameness. Like dissolving into some bland spiritual mush where individuality disappeared. That never sat right with me.

But now I saw it clearly: oneness isn't sameness. Oneness is unity. We don't become the same, instead we drop the illusions that divide us. We let go of judgment, of the need to prove, fix, or convert. We stop believing "other" means separate. We retain our individuality. What makes us unique is celebrated.

True unity embraces every difference. It doesn't erase us; it amplifies us. In oneness, we become even more ourselves. More vibrant. More alive. More authentic!

We are not One. We are *everything*.

Each of us is a unique expression of the same divine spark, each with full access to the infinite.

Losing our identity? That would be a tragedy. The whole point is to become more of who we are: to be lit up, turned on, fully expressed! That's love. That's the real unity. Not a melting down, but a rising up, neon, loud, expressive and unapologetically authentic!

As that knowing sank in, my heart cracked open. My forehead still buzzed with light. A car behind me honked, and I snapped back into the moment. I pressed the gas and moved forward, with every other version of me, each of us driving our own story home.

Chapter Forty-Two

Is it Nudges or Noise?

I knew I needed to trust my intuition, but what was intuition and what was just me? How would I know what was a nudge of divine guidance and what was my mind sending me in circles? Sometimes the nudges felt inspired, but I had other urges guiding me: my fears, my sense of obligation, logical and illogical worry. I had to learn how to tell the difference. Sometimes my mind was able to convince me I had some magical insight when really, I was just catastrophizing.

I started reading into everything. What does it mean? What is the universe telling me? It was sending me in circles. It wasn't sustainable. It was paralyzing.

So, I decided instead of questioning everything I needed to figure out what was a nudge and what was noise. To tell the difference I had to give myself some boundaries. So, I decided as long as the hunch wasn't going to hurt someone, be illegal, or cost money, I would follow it.

Call someone out of the blue? Go for it. Buy new furniture because I saw the same advertisement on social media three times? Not a nudge.

The next time my intuition tested me was in the middle of the night on a warm summer evening after my daughter graduated high school. I woke up at 2am and looked at my phone to see the time. As was my habit, I also checked the locations for my kids. With college only a couple months away, I'd removed my daughter's curfew. Most nights, when I looked at my phone, it showed her in her room, so I would go right back to sleep. But this time when I looked at my phone, it showed her in the ocean.

We lived at the beach so while it was unlikely she was in the ocean, it wasn't impossible. Was this a nudge from intuition? Did I wake up because my daughter is in danger?

Being half awake didn't help my discernment. I remembered my promise to myself that if there wasn't anything bad that would come from the nudge, I would follow it to see if it was real. So, I put my shoes on and a sweatshirt over my pajamas and drove to the beach to save my daughter from drowning in the ocean at 2 am.

It was a gorgeous night. The moon was full, and the stars were twinkling.

I turned on the flashlight on my phone and trudged toward the water in my boots, watching the circle of my location on the app get closer to my daughter's circle. In the dark, I saw some people on a blanket up ahead and could hear them talking.

"Eliza?" I said loudly, approaching the group of people in the spot that the app now showed my daughter on the beach.

An uncertain voice replied, "Mom?"

There was no disappearing now. I had to fully commit. I had driven to the beach in the middle of the night for nothing. My daughter wasn't drowning, she was hanging out with her friends. I stepped closer and lit my face with my phone's flashlight. I tried to act casual.

"Oh, hi," I said, approaching the group. "It's a pretty night to be out here."

"Mom, what are you doing?"

"I'm being an idiot obviously. I'm sorry. I woke up and looked at your location and it looked like you were in the ocean, so I came out to save you."

"Oh my God, that is so cute," her friend said.

It didn't feel cute to me, it felt like I was humiliating my daughter.

"I'm sorry, Eliza," I saw your location and it looked like you were in the ocean. I thought if I didn't come and something happened to you, I'd never forgive myself. But if I did come, and you were fine, you'd never forgive me. So, here we are."

"It's fine, Mom," she said.

"Hi, are these your friends?" I gestured toward the boys in the group.

We defaulted into the polite formality of young people meeting a parent. The boys introduced themselves and extended their hands for me to shake. "Nice to meet you," I introduced myself.

Her friend Tracy stood up to give me a hug. "This is honestly the funniest thing. I totally get you. I think my mom would do the same thing!"

I knew Tracy from countless times at my house lounging in the living room or in my daughter's room as they planned out their days and listened to music.

"It was probably your apple watch," Tracy said to Eliza, "We were swimming earlier."

Then she turned to me, "We were being very safe though. We weren't going out too far."

"I'm going to go home now. I'm glad you are having fun and being safe."

Eliza got up and gave me a hug. "I love you mom. You need more sleep."

I trudged back to my car, embarrassed but, now I knew. That one wasn't an intuitive hit. It was just a mom moment.

While it was embarrassing, it also helped me get really clear on another aspect of my intuition. When I got a download of information in the car, or washing dishes like it always came with a sensation like my body and mind was on pause, where everything internally and externally was slowed down or completely still. If it came with worry, it *was* worry and probably better left alone.

Chapter Forty-Three

Radical Delusion

I was learning an entirely new way to experience the world. Things were getting clearer in my mind. I had ways of understanding things and making decisions that hadn't been available to me previously, but there were still so many questions, chief among them, *Was I a medium? And if I was, how would I know?*

"You'll just have to try to do it and see what happens," Jae said when I asked her. "Find people who will let you practice with them. See if the faces show up or if anything else happens when you are with them. You can practice with me. I've lost a lot of people who you don't know about."

"This just seems so crazy," I continued. "How can I be sure this isn't just a massive delusion?"

"Your therapist said you aren't crazy," Jae reminded me. "And I don't think you're crazy, either. I just think you're stubborn."

"You aren't wrong about that," I conceded. "It's very hard for me to believe talking to dead people is real."

"Why," Jae shot back. "It's not like you are some unshakable voice of reason. It's not like you are the sound of logic in all things. You believe crazy things all the time. I've seen you believe things that are far crazier than this without even blinking."

"Like what?" I asked, accusing her.

"You believed Gunther would change. You believed he didn't know what he was doing would hurt you," she shot back. "You believed if you worked hard and put in extra hours, management would notice you and give you a promotion."

I was silently fuming but still listening because she was right. She continued, relentlessly.

"You believed you were the problem. You believed you weren't good enough. You believe you don't have talent as a writer. You believed there was something wrong with you. Despite all the evidence, you keep on fucking believing the craziest shit! You are the most delusional person I've ever known!"

My eyes had welled up with tears. I wanted to cry but needed to laugh.

"You're such a bitch," I said, laughing and wiping away tears.

When I said that, she let out a laugh too.

"Well, it's true."

We both took a moment to take it all in. She had said so much. She must have been holding it all in for so long.

Jae said, "You can believe anything you want. So, why not believe in yourself."

She was right. I was able to believe anything if I chose to and most of the time, if I was being honest, my beliefs were based on choice and nothing more. I believed unbelievable things because I didn't want to feel the discomfort or loss from seeing the truth. I believed things that kept me small and stuck because it was familiar. To create a new life, I needed to have new beliefs. I needed to believe in myself, and in the amazing future waiting for me. I didn't even have to know how I would get there I just needed to believe that I would. This, this ability to believe absolutely anything no matter how delusional it seemed, was something I was already really good at.

Chapter Forty-Four

Anything Is Possible

I still wasn't sure if I was really a medium. I'd been listening to podcasts by Suzanne Giesemann. She's a former U.S. Navy Commander who served as a commanding officer and aide to the Chairman of the Joint Chiefs of Staff before becoming an evidential medium. The death of her stepdaughter inspired her to pursue connecting with the afterlife. With persistence and patience, she was able to do it. She taught herself how to connect with the other side and then has been teaching others to do it as well. I was drawn to her because of her prestigious career and methodical mind. If someone like Suzanne whose entire career and reputation was built on reason and logic could trust the unseen, then I could too.

I was opening up to more friends to tell them about my experience and was surprised to find not only that they didn't think it was that weird but that they'd had their own inexplicable experiences themselves.

I hadn't seen my friend Adrienne since the night I shit myself in the Wendy's parking lot. I knew she would be someone I could tell. She was both grounded and open-minded, but I was surprised when she told me she had always been interested in psychic abilities, the unknown and had even been to mediums before with her sister.

For as well as I thought I knew some of my friends, I was finding there were things that had never come up, aspects of ourselves we had never shared before. I wondered if I was that good of a friend if I only knew a portion of their lives. How was I missing so much?

A couple of days after I told Adrienne about my experience, she called me. "Theresa Caputo is coming to town in three days!"

"Who is that!?" I asked. She sounded so excited. I wanted to share her excitement.

"The Long Island Medium!"

"Oh!" My response was just vague enough Adrienne could tell I still didn't know who she was talking about.

"Have you heard of her?"

"No, but you sound excited, so I'll look her up!"

"Are you free on Thursday?"

"Yes!"

"I'm buying us tickets. No need to look her up. We will see her together!"

A couple weeks later, we were in the balcony seats at the Wilson Center in downtown Wilmington, NC. As Theresa worked the stage, I watched her with a strange mix of awe and certainty. During the event, Theresa walked to people in the audience. She gave them evidence and messages from spirit. She drilled into details. The people in the audience were moved to tears. They held each other's hands to try to stay steady with the experience. It was overwhelming in a beautiful way.

I knew I could do what Theresa was doing. I didn't know how, but it was a recognition in me. It was like I was feeling the same information Teresa was sharing. I couldn't articulate it like she could, and couldn't describe how I knew, but I could feel it in my body that there was a way for me to do this too. If Suzanne Giesemann could teach herself, I could too.

I read the book "Medium Mentor" by MaryAnn DiMarco. After reading it, I decided I should find a mentor myself. I looked up MaryAnn's website. The fees to study with her were thousands of dollars. I searched for other mediums who might offer mentorship and found the same thing: a mentor would cost thousands. I had to find another way. I needed more than just theory; I needed to do it. That was the only way I would find out, by diving in.

Finally, I found a class online for a Mediumship 101 class taught by an Evidential Medium named Heather Visnesky. She lived close to my parents' house, and I liked that there was a possibility that I could someday meet her in person. Her class was only a couple hundred dollars and taught completely online. She looked to be about my age and like me, she was juggling a full-time job, family and kids. Most importantly, in her bio she didn't describe herself as having these abilities her whole life but, like me she discovered them later in life unexpectedly.

I had twelve laying hens in my flock. They were laying more eggs than I could eat or even sell. If I sold eight of them, I could pay for her class. I signed up immediately.

I'd have to wait a few weeks for class to start. But once I made the decision to really dive in and give it a shot, I got impatient. I wanted to start immediately. Once I get an idea in my head, I can't think of anything else until I start. I've never been one to make a careful plan. I leap and then I figure it out later.

My friend Katie agreed to let me practice with her. She promised to be one hundred percent honest and to never tell anyone what we did if it turned out I was just a middle-aged woman having a breakdown.

I was surprised by her openness and encouragement. I wondered if I would have been as supportive if the roles were reversed. I'd like to think I would have been but in truth, I was realizing that of all the people who knew about my new interest in things like mediumship, clairvoyance, visitation dreams, and psychic abilities, the harshest judgment had been my own. I was the one who had believed it was all fake. I was the one who questioned the sanity, or intelligence, of anyone exploring anything that couldn't be proven by science. Even when friends volunteered to help or shared their own experiences, my first instinct wasn't gratitude...it was suspicion. Could I trust them? Were they making it up? And the irony was, I was the one who brought it up in the first place.

I set my laptop up on my bed instead of at my desk. I was afraid to change anything in case I'd imprinted my spiritual gifts on the small patch of space where I sat when I meditated. I saw the notification that she had joined the zoom and took a deep breath.

Immediately my chest started to tingle.

"I don't know if I'm just nervous, but my chest is tingling," I said, laughing.

"So is mine!" she said.

I saw a big house on a hill with kids playing on the front lawn. It was an idyllic scene that I was familiar with, a blend between a house I'd seen in a movie and one I'd imagined.

"I've seen this house before," I said. "It's actually like the house of my dreams for when I am older. So, I don't know if this is my imagination but I'm just going to say everything."

"Sounds like a good plan," Katie said.

"It's this big house on a hill and the house is white and the hill goes down to the left. I feel like I'm approaching from a long driveway on the right. I feel like there's a gravel driveway, the gravel that is grey pebbles. And there are a lot of kids around. They don't feel like they live there. The kids are visiting."

"Yes," Katie said. "I think I know who this is. We went to her house for holidays."

My lips started to tingle, like I'd blotted them with rubbing alcohol. "Was she talkative? Easy to talk to?"

Katie confirmed this was true.

Next, it felt like a camera was zooming in closer to the house and I saw a woman standing on the porch. "I see a woman standing on the front porch. She looks friendly and loving. She is wearing a long skirt. She looks comfortable. I see the number 72. Does that mean anything to you?"

"I think that is my aunt," she says. "I will need to think about 72. It's a maybe."

"I see flowers, not real flowers but patterns of flowers to decorate with. And I'm getting the sense she loved to make a house a home. She loved to take care of the house and her family."

"Yes, that makes sense," Katie said.

"She's showing me an angel," I said, seeing a stone garden angel. "But it's not a decoration. She's telling me she's your guardian angel." The ideas were coming to my mind like thoughts, but they felt like they didn't originate from me. "And she's telling me you're her angel too. You give her hope. You're her light."

Katie explained that after a car accident several years ago, she could feel her aunt's presence protecting her. "I felt like she was there, and she had somehow prevented the accident from being worse."

"She said you're like a daughter to her. She's rocking a baby. You are precious to her."

Katie confirmed that was true—her mother had told her this after her aunt's passing.

"There's a man with her now," I said. "He's just popping in to say hello. He's got white hair and glasses."

"That's my uncle."

I almost dismissed the detail as too vague but then I focused on his thick, white hair. It was a detail I couldn't have known, so I mentioned it.

"He likes to get things done. Works hard and stays busy with projects. I feel like he's more working outside and she's inside." Then I felt a shift that got my attention. "Hold on, I feel like he wants me to phrase that differently. He says, while he's just popping in now, he wants you to know he is right by your aunt. He's put his arm around her at the shoulders as if to show 'She's right here with me.'"

"That's great," Katie said.

"Did he pass first?" I asked. "It feels like he welcomed her there." I couldn't even explain how I knew to say that. It was the feeling of him putting his arm around her and pulling her close. Did I see that? Or did I feel it?

"Yes, he passed first," Katie confirmed.

After that I felt like I was straining. My energy was drained. I wondered if Katie was just being nice. She wouldn't have lied to me, but maybe the evidence was very vague and could apply to anyone. Surely everyone's aunt is nice and loved them. An aunt who loved flowers. And an uncle who passed first. It wasn't completely general, but it did not feel specific. For it to be meaningful, it would have to be specific.

The one detail that stood out to me was her uncle's thick, bright white hair. That seemed specific. Not many men had hair at all by his age but to have a thick head of white hair was specific. It was the kind of detail that would get a definite yes or no. It wasn't subjective. That's the kind of evidence I wanted to get in my readings, and I wanted to get a lot of it.

Chapter Forty-Five

Glinda is Real (ish)

I decided to take a leave of absence from grad school. I was feeling stretched thin and the only thing I wanted to think about was how there was more to the world and consciousness than I had realized. I wanted to know what else was possible. I was learning about Reiki, Astrology, sound healing, the quantum field and the Akashic Records. I was meditating every chance I could get. If I could sneak in twenty minutes of quiet and deep breathing, I would. I noticed my stress was reducing. At work, instead of getting overwhelmed, I'd stop myself before reacting to an urgent or aggressive email. I'd sit back in my chair, breathe in through my nose and exhale through my mouth.

"Everything is going to be okay," I'd tell myself. Often, by the time I went back to the task, someone else had responded, or the email looked different to me. What I had interpreted as an aggressive tone was only urgency and stress.

The environment was high pressure. There was an undercurrent of anxiety and stress in every meeting. If I could step back and slow down the momentum of anxiety, even just for myself, we might all benefit.

Was I really trying to get an advanced degree so that I could have *more* of this? The corporate management strategies I was supposed to be studying couldn't hold my attention compared to the world that was opening before me. How could I focus on organizational hierarchies and profit margins when meditation, mysticism, shamanism, crystals, and sacred geometry were calling to me?

I gave myself six months to go deep into all things spiritual before going back to school. A soul sabbatical. Then I promised myself I would return to finish the degree.

The one class I was excited about was Heather Visnesky's Mediumship 101 class. Students were from all over, so we met on Zoom. Some had been mediums since childhood, seeing spirit as naturally as breathing. Others, like me, were just beginning to explore abilities they'd either ignored or never realized they had. Our teacher assured us that we all possess these gifts inherently, but like any skill, they require practice to refine. Even the lifelong mediums were there to sharpen their connection.

I arrived ready to dive straight into the exciting stuff: connecting with spirits, delivering messages, exploring the mysteries of the afterlife. But our first class wasn't about any of that. It was about ethics.

"Ethics, professionalism, and evidence are the three pillars of evidential mediumship," our teacher explained. I felt a mix of impatience and respect. I wanted to get to the supernatural part, but I understood why this foundation mattered.

"There's plenty of space to be wrong," our teacher assured us. "Mediumship is subtle. You'll make mistakes. But you must have integrity. You must be honest. You must hold yourself to high standards."

I was riveted. "This work is an honor," she said. "It is sacred."

The following week, we moved into the practical aspects of mediumship—learning how to pay attention to two different worlds simultaneously. It's like patting your head and rubbing your stomach in circles at the same time, maintaining two conversations at once: one spoken with the living person in front of you, and one silent, in your mind, with the spirit world.

At first, I could only focus on one realm at a time. When I tried to connect with spirit, I'd retreat deep into my mind, waiting for images to appear before describing them. It felt like sitting by a radio, waiting for messages to come through static. During one practice session, I sat for twenty minutes and received only three vague pictures. The other students were patient, but inside I was squirming. It felt like an eternity of awkward silence. When we gave each other feedback, nothing

I'd described resonated with anyone. My "messages" were just my imagination at work.

I thought back to my reading with Katie. Had that been real? Or just a lucky coincidence?

By the final week of the workshop, we'd progressed to full practice readings, treating them like official sessions. We introduced ourselves professionally, gave a brief explanation of how mediumship works, and, crucially, asked for consent before attempting to connect with their loved ones. Our teacher taught us consent was just as important as integrity. Having a message for someone doesn't automatically give you the right to deliver it. You can't just rush up to strangers in the grocery store with impromptu communications from their deceased relatives.

My practice professional reading left me discouraged. I saw Glinda the Good Witch from The Wizard of Oz floating before my mind's eye, complete with puffy pink dress and magic wand. Obviously, my sitter wasn't related to a fictional character.

"Say whatever you get. Don't overthink it."

"Uh, I'm seeing the good witch from wizard of Oz, so, um, I guess was there someone you watched this movie with? Maybe it's a special memory?"

"No," she said.

I tried to feel into more information but came up blank. "That's all," I said. "I think I'm getting in my head."

"Try again, it's okay. We are all practicing. There's no grades."

"Okay."

There was nothing. Just emptiness. After a couple minutes, I opened my eyes. "I don't think I'm getting anything."

We each took a turn. The more experienced mediums shared everything. If they saw one image they would describe it in detail, like they were turning it around to show it from all sides. They didn't just describe a car, they described the color, make and model. they described if it was new or old. It seemed like the more they shared, the more information they received.

When it was time for feedback, I braced myself. I felt like I had done terribly.

"Glinda is my spirit guide," one of the students said, her face lighting up.

I blinked, trying to process her words. Glinda. The Good Witch. A spirit guide?

Our teacher explained that spirit guides can be anything, real or fictional, because spirit doesn't operate on rigid definitions of what's "real" or "imagined." Spirit speaks in symbols, archetypes, subconscious images, even pop culture references. It's the language of the psyche. Deeply personal. Deeply resonant.

"I think your reading was for me," said one of the other students. Not the one I was reading for.

"Spirit guides are often conscious constructs, energetic beings born from intention, emotion, repetition, and belief. The quantum field doesn't respond to matter; it responds to coherence. The more focused and emotionally charged the attention, the stronger the imprint.

I began to understand. Glinda wasn't just a character. She was an archetype, shaped by decades of collective resonance and lit up by personal significance. She wasn't "real" in the physical sense, but in the energetic sense, she absolutely was. Her archetype offered exactly the support my classmate needed. I had tapped into it. She recognized it.

Where attention goes, energy flows.

Then I thought of the strings between me and others, between everything. Invisible, but alive. Energy-filled. The more attention we give something, the stronger it gets. Every connection is a current. Every thought, a thread. Even connections to stories, ideas and characters. Our collective attention creates the field we all live in. It becomes the unconscious we share.

I thought of the pin with strings between them, but this time it looked more like a cat's cradle, each of us connected in some way and pulling on each other with more tension sometimes, more slack other times. Everything is connected in every direction.

Chapter Forty-Six

Every Reality is Valid

E ven though I wasn't getting the specific details I wanted in my practice readings, I was getting something. It made me want more. I was hungry. I needed people to let me practice with them, mostly to prove to myself over and over that it was real. And if it was real, then I was sane. And if I was sane, then this feeling of comfort might be lasting.

"What do you think if I host an event and invite people to sit while I read spirit for them?" I asked my son one evening.

"That's not even real, Mom," he told me in a tone that felt like the roles had reversed, and he was parenting me very sternly while I lived in my playhouse.

"It is real," I said.

He gave me the side eye. I didn't need to convince him. I didn't even want to. I respected his perspective. After all, hadn't I been just as skeptical before my own experiences? My son approached the world with caution and critical thinking. He observed, analyzed, and made his judgments based on evidence, qualities I'd always encouraged in him. Now these very traits created a boundary between us that I had to honor.

"Listen, whether it's real or not, I'm trying to grow and make friends. It makes me happy."

"It's fine," he said. "Just don't invite my friends' parents." This was a fair boundary. It gave me space to explore and gave him protection from judgment or criticism from his own circle.

He had enough to navigate without his mother being known as the local medium. The contrast between my son's skepticism and my emerging abilities created a strange dynamic in our home. He could sense the positive changes in me. I was calmer, more present, less anxious, and he appreciated these differences.

But whenever I mentioned a spirit interaction, a reading or an intuitive hit, he was quick to remind me flatly, with his deep voice that he didn't believe in it.

"You might be right," I said. "And I might be right too." He was skeptical. "But what's the harm in me believing what I believe as long as it doesn't interfere with you and what you believe. Can we just both believe our things, side by side?"

We agreed to coexist with mutual respect. Silence didn't mean agreement, but agreement wasn't necessary. We only needed freedom.

Sometimes love meant giving space for different truths to coexist. His reality was just as valid as mine, a lesson we were living in my house, every day.

Chapter Forty-Seven

Ancestral Ties

A few weeks later, I was able to attend a practice group in person. It was called a Spirit Circle. It was an informal gathering of spiritually open people to connect and practice their gifts. You could practice tarot, energy reading, mediumship or just come to talk about things you'd been sensing or curious about. There were six of us, all from different backgrounds but wanting to find ways to connect more deeply with others and with ourselves.

There was a stay-at-home mom, a lawyer, a real estate agent, a teacher, a graphic designer and me. We all introduced ourselves, shared our experience with spirituality and our goals for the evening. I told the group I was trying to figure out if I was a medium. I said I had done some practice readings for friends and took a couple classes, but I wasn't consistently getting information to suggest I was a medium.

"I might be a medium," I said. "I'm not sure."

They offered to let me do the first reading. One person named Alex in the group volunteered to be the recipient.

I asked for her consent then closed my eyes and immediately saw a face so close to my own it startled me. Every detail was vivid. She had golden brown skin weathered into deep wrinkles; dark braids streaked with gray, impossibly high cheekbones. The face appeared genderless, but I sensed a feminine energy, strong, determined, forceful yet kind. *This couldn't be someone related to Alex,* I thought. She was light skinned, light haired. She didn't have any Native American features and the spirit I was connecting to was clearly Native American. *This must be her spirit guide*, I thought. Maybe I wasn't a medium. Maybe I just connected with guides.

I described her features anyway. Then a cold sensation washed over my teeth, as if my own teeth were gone.

"Her teeth are all missing," I noted.

"Yes," Alex confirmed.

The instructions for a reading are for the person to only say "yes," "no," or "I don't know," so that they don't give too much leading information.

Everything I shared about this spirit, the number of children she had, the conflicts in her life, her personality, resulted in a "yes." Surely, I was getting some of this wrong. Surely, I was just making it up. In addition to seeing this woman's features, I also felt the familiar urging of wanting to say something personal. The same urging I felt when James was on the road trip with his daughter.

Just let it go, Kathryn. I said to myself. *Don't think, just speak.*

"She's telling you to hang on. She says you have been born into conflict and experience resistance, but you are bringing in the new ways. She also faced a lot of resistance. She knows what you are going through and she is rooting for you. She is always with you. She was vocal and outspoken, just like you are, and she knows the pain that brings but she wants you to keep going. She was unconventional. Was she exiled?" I asked this last question, shocking even myself. What a strange but specific thing to bring up.

"Yes," the sitter said.

"Don't give up, don't give up." The urgent message was so strong.

I took a deep breath, opened my eyes and looked around the room. Alex was wiping tears away from her cheeks.

"That's my grandmother," she said, her voice cracking with emotion.

A wave of wonder crashed over me. I had seen her grandmother. I had felt her presence. She had communicated through me in the same way Julie had. I felt the merging of our energy. I recognized what it felt like.

"I have wanted her to come through so many times and she never has until now," she said.

She pulled a picture from her wallet. We passed it around. The woman was exactly as I'd described.

While I sat there, I felt so close to Alex. I felt protective of her. I wanted to hug her. I wanted to give her more. I wasn't just feeling my own emotions; I was feeling the love from her grandmother. I wanted to say, "I love you," in the same way I'd said "I love you" to James. They weren't my words, but I was a messenger for them.

Mediumship had become about proof for me. Proving that life continues after death. Proving that it was real. Proving that I wasn't crazy. Proving that the spirit world exists. But now I saw it was more than that. It was about connection and communication. I was delivering messages from another time, from another realm that desperately needed to be delivered.

Mediumship wasn't only about the afterlife; it was about this life that we're still living. It was about giving people something they needed so they could keep going, to give them clarity, comfort or encouragement when they needed it most.

"You're definitely a medium," Alex said, still wiping tears from her eyes.

The others agreed and chuckled, as if my uncertainty was laughable now.

Everyone started to talk and share. The mood shifted to a social event; others shared their experiences. A woman pulled cards; we did a joint meditation.

But I still felt Alex's grandmother with me. I felt like I wanted to say more. I didn't know how to handle it, so I stayed quiet.

That night, I couldn't sleep. I replayed the reading in my mind. I saw the wrinkles; I remembered the teeth.

Then, I saw her face in front of me again, as close and vivid as it was before.

"Thank you," she said. I could feel her deep gratitude.

"You're welcome." I said back, meaning it.

"This is for you," she said. She handed me something small wrapped in velvet. When I opened it, I saw the web of ancestry. I saw the strings of light again, connecting us each but this time I saw how some strings that connect us to ancestors are stronger than others. Even in the same family, there might be someone a generation or more back in our family line who has a large, bright string attached to us. Our connections defy time or generations.

This grandmother's bond with her granddaughter was one of those. It had skipped a generation, bypassed convention, and anchored itself in something deeper. They didn't look alike. They didn't live the same life. But they shared the same *energy*. The same contracts. The same purpose. They were *twins*, separated only by time.

The message needed to be delivered as much as it needed to be received. That was the force I had felt. The feeling of urgency, the insistence, the desire for connection. It was love.

All the structures I'd once believed in suddenly felt too small, too linear. Everything was energy. Our connections weren't just sentimental, they were *structural*. They created the scaffolding of lifetimes.

I wondered what my own ancestral connections meant before finally closing my eyes to sleep.

Chapter Forty-Eight

VerySoul

A few weeks later, I was talking to my friend Heather who taught Mediumship 101. I was giving her an update on my progress and asking for her perspective on some recent experiences. During our call, she asked, "Have you ever heard of VerySoul?"

"No, what's that?" I was intrigued.

"It's an online platform designed to destigmatize mediumship by making it both more credible and more accessible. It was founded by medium Sally Hawk with the support of Suzanne Giesemann. You can practice there with other mediums as much as you want. And it's free to join."

"Anyone can join? Even beginners?"

"Yes, anyone who can get a link to a spirit," Heather told me. "But to advance to the next level, you have to be vetted. Or you can stay in the practice level forever. It's up to you."

This was exactly what I needed. Finding willing practice partners had been my biggest obstacle. Friends were either too skeptical or too supportive, neither giving me the objective feedback I needed.

"You can practice with strangers who understand what you're doing," Heather continued. "And since they're also mediums they'll be honest about what's accurate and patient while you grow."

I signed up immediately. Within 48 hours, I was fully onboarded and giving my first reading to someone I'd never met. The impact was immediate and profound.

No more begging friends for practice sessions. No more wondering if they were just being nice. Just open the website, find an available slot, and connect. Sometimes I'd do three readings in a day, practicing different techniques with each one. I'd try to use only clairsentience, I'd push myself to focus on the manner of death, the personality or relationship.

Once again, the promises were being fulfilled. I have everything I need. I always have more than enough. The universe had provided the perfect platform at the perfect time, without costing me a dime. I just had to show up.

Chapter Forty-Nine

Creating Space

One of the first practice readings I gave on VerySoul was for a young woman who was hiding in her closet.

Not metaphorically. She was literally sitting in a closet in her house, hiding from her three kids. Her husband was watching them so she could have a moment of quiet for the reading, but she knew, as moms always do, that if her kids heard her voice on the phone, they'd come barging in. She was also a medium, so we were going to take an hour to practice together, first would be my turn and then hers.

The moment I connected to spirit, I saw a young man in a photograph with his arm around someone, smiling wide, full of life. Then suddenly, I got hot. My whole body started burning up. I saw the same young man in a hospital bed, drenched in sweat, in terrible pain but also above his body. Watching.

I described everything just as I saw it. A part of me wondered if I should stop. It felt too graphic, especially when she started to cry. But the evidence was so clear, so strong. I didn't want to miss any of it. So, I let it flow.

He showed me that he had already left his body, even while it was still alive and writhing in pain. It was no longer usable, and he knew death was inevitable. When there was a natural pause in the flow, I checked in with her gently.

"I'm so sorry. Do you want me to continue?"

"Yes," she said. "Please."

He continued to show me the fever, the confusion, the physical discomfort of his final days. He had been sick for a while. At some point, he stepped out of his body, partly from curiosity, partly from shock. Outside of it, he understood what was happening.

And then, peace.

He showed me the most profound peace. No more pain from the illness. No more pain from life. He had loved many people but had often felt isolated, like he was going through the motions. He hadn't wanted to fight anymore. And somehow, even though his passing was unexpected, he had been ready.

"This is your brother," I said gently. "Is your brother in spirit?"

"Yes," she said through tears.

I didn't know how to hold her grief in that moment. It's not my job to counsel, just to be the bridge. But the love between them was palpable.

She told me he had passed in November in the Philippines. He'd been working there as an English teacher and died from sepsis. The family wasn't even notified for several weeks. They kept reaching out with no response, until her father received a letter from the embassy: his body was taking up space and needed to be collected.

That was the first they'd heard he was even sick, let alone deceased.

From there, it was a mind-numbing journey for her family. They were working through translators and government agencies trying to piece together what had happened. All they knew was that he had told the concierge at his apartment that he was sick. The concierge called him a car to the hospital. He passed just a couple days later.

"He's okay now," I told her. "He's right here with you."

"How do you know that?" she asked. "What are you seeing to show you that?"

I looked again with my third eye and saw her sitting just as she was—in the closet. But now with her brother beside her, wearing a goofy grin and giving her an awkward air hug.

"This is random, but I've got to say it. He's showing himself giving you an awkward air hug, like his arm is halfway around you and he's got this goofy look on his face." I mimicked the smile and the air hug.

She laughed through tears. "That's exactly how he was! He was sort of awkward! And his smile was goofy just like that!"

Then I saw him again. This time he was at her kitchen island. The kids were watching TV or playing, and he was sitting at the island while she cooked. He was keeping an eye on everyone at once. He felt at home. Welcomed. Connected. Part of the family.

She said, "I could sit here with you forever. I can feel him here. You described him perfectly."

Then she told me something I needed to hear.

"I'm so glad you told me everything about his passing. It must have been so awful for him to be alone and in that pain. No one was with him... but everything you said aligns with what we read in the documents. He had sepsis, a high fever, delusions, and was in tremendous pain. They treated him with antibiotics and very high doses of pain medication, which he must have needed.

"If you hadn't been so detailed and accurate about his death," she said. "It would have been harder to believe the comforting messages. They feel too good to be true. To think he's okay now and here. But I believe it. I believe it because everything else lined up. And I can feel that it's true."

"You just changed my life," she said. "I feel so much better. I know he's here. I can feel him too. Thank you so much."

Chapter Fifty

The Refinished Basement

E ven though I could see the healing that mediumship was offering for others, I didn't think I needed it myself. I wanted to give readings, not receive them. Many of the mediums I practiced with had started their journey because they lost someone they couldn't live without. Like Suzanne Giesemann, they'd intentionally trained to develop the sensitivity. Or like me, they'd had a dream of their loved one coming to visit. There were so many reasons for people to pursue mediumship, but everyone had one thing in common. We all knew how important it was. We all knew that a single reading could change someone's life for the better. We all knew we were healing hearts and souls on both sides with this ability, and we were committed to doing it with the highest integrity, highest standard of evidence and the biggest hearts possible.

While I had witnessed the healing many times, I had never been a recipient of it. I had friends and family come through in my practice readings but none of my lost ones had devastated me. My grandparents passed in their later years and after an illness. Their passing seemed timely, and even a gift to end suffering. Others had passed but often I'd heard about their passing after we'd lost touch. My losses didn't leave a gaping hole in my heart like it did for others.

I didn't think I needed healing. It was enough for me to witness theirs. Then, in one of my practice sessions with another medium on Very Soul, I received a profound message that gave me both insight and comfort.

It was a regular Saturday, and I'd set myself up in front of my laptop to give reading after reading, working to refine my connection to get stronger and stronger evidence.

To give a message we build the energy with spirit and the sitter

We trust spirit to decide who comes through. Sometimes the sitter has a need, sometimes spirit has a need. Sometimes the link is with someone with a strong energetic match to the medium.

We bring forward evidence that you will recognize.

I had the script down.

The recent readings I'd given were fair, but I wanted them to be great. Likewise, the readings I'd received were fair, but the mediums kept mentioning a man in a shed or garage with a lot of tools who I didn't recognize. It sounded both like someone still alive and also like no one in particular. It was too general. But because he kept coming up in reading after reading, I knew it must be someone. But who?

Then in my last reading of the day, it became clear. The medium said, "This is random, but I've got to say it. He's showing me a refinished basement."

And immediately, I knew who it was. It was Wayne, my old roommate from Seattle. My ex-husband and I lived in Seattle in our twenties. We rented a bedroom from an older couple named Wayne and Ruth. They lived in a refinished basement, and we lived on the second floor. We shared the common areas on the first floor. Ruth had multiple sclerosis that was relapsing. They were so in love, but her illness was taking a toll on them mentally, financially and physically.

One night, while my ex, our roommates and I were watching a movie in the living room, Wayne and Ruth decided to end their suffering. She took sleeping pills and then he shot her in the head and then himself. Their letters of apology and explanation showed up three days later.

We were in shock. Now, almost thirty years later, Wayne, avid gardener, handy man and homestyle cook had been trying to say something to me for weeks. Finally, he had a medium who had a memory in her bank that he could use as evidence to connect to me. The refinished basement. I needed that detail to make the connection to link the evidence to him and no one else could do it but the medium working with me now. And that piece made the link undeniable.

His message to me?

"Did you build something? He's showing you standing on a roof and using power tools. I don't know what that means. He's showing you in a heroic stance." She held her arms up in the air with her hands in fists celebrating an achievement. Gunther had taken a picture of me standing on the roof of the coop in that very pose after I'd drilled in the bolts.

"I know what that means," I said. "He saw me building the chicken coop."

"Yes," she confirmed. "That makes sense now with what I'm seeing. He says he can see how far you've come. He says you work too much!"

"Thank you. Thank you, Wayne!"

Chapter Fifty-One

The Fearless Medium

Every time I took a chance with mediumship, I felt seen, like I had a purpose. So, I decided to rent a small event space near my house, invite all my friends and give a demonstration of mediumship for the crowd, just like Theresa Caputo. My birthday had never been that special to me. I'd never really done anything to celebrate it. Most years, it was forgotten by everyone, including me. But it was a great excuse to invite my friends to get together, so I could share everything I had been talking about with them. I would host a demonstration of mediumship.

I made a list of everyone I thought might come, told them I would have cupcakes and asked them to attend. It felt just like it did when I was a kid and my family would go to the living room after eating a big holiday meal. I would turn on Olivia Newton John on the record player and dance an improvisational routine while aunts, uncles and grandparents were held captive in their chairs. I spun and kicked my way around the room in my spandex pants and sequined off the shoulder flash dance style tee shirt. Except for the dancing and spandex, it was just like that.

I knew I could connect to spirit. I'd been doing it on VerySoul with increasing consistency. Now, I would just have do it in a room with ten people sitting around. It wouldn't be that different, would it?

Twelve friends showed up, two brought more friends with them. Some were skeptical but willing to suspend disbelieve because I asked them. Most were eager.

The folding chairs were laid out theater style, I played a song from my phone, introduced myself like a professional and then began the readings.

All I could feel was my own nervous system freaking out from standing in front of a bunch of my friends to accomplish something unbelievable that I claimed to be able to do. I was so nervous I was almost shaking.

I took a deep breath, felt into my energy. Come on, Kathryn. Get out of the way. I didn't sense any spirits present. It was still just me buzzing chaotically. I was back to the beginning, grasping for a single piece of evidence, being met with a "no." The visuals were so faint and far I couldn't tell what I saw.

I was grasping. I started to throw out evidence that was general. It was weak. It could be anyone. My friends were generous. They tried to make it match, but it didn't. They were patient. They sat there while I struggled. They smiled.

"Keep going," one friend said.

"You've got this!"

I took a deep breath and exhaled with my eyes closed. "I can do this," I told myself.

I saw a man leaning against a motorcycle. He had his arms crossed but wore a smirk. He was early fifties, slender and charming. It still felt too vague, but it was something, so I shared it.

Two of my friends thought maybe, just maybe. So, I continued.

He has dark hair and he's flirtatious, He's got a "Hey Baby" vibe so maybe he was a romantic partner, not a family member.

He's saying, "You're so sexy, baby." We all chuckled.

"Something happened to his head. Horrible headaches. A terrible, fast, devastating illness."

One of the two dropped out. That didn't resonate, but it made sense for the other one. I spent forty-five minutes, just for that? It was going to have to be good enough for me. I had to stay positive. I couldn't let the "no's" get me into my head.

The next two links didn't resonate with anyone. I moved on quickly but was getting tired. My body was slowly aching. I didn't want to keep them here forever.

Finally, I lost my patience and yelled at the spirit in my mind, "Come on! You wanted me to do this! I didn't choose it! You chose me, so show up!"

In all my mediumship classes, I'd been taught to approach the spirit world with deep reverence, waiting for them to share whatever they felt like. I wasn't supposed to demand things; I was supposed to receive.

Here I was demanding they show up. "I booked this room for you! I invited all my friends for you! And now I'm standing up here making an ass out of myself. Don't you dare leave me hanging! Show up now!"

Immediately, I saw a dark street in the rain, trees overhanging, moonlight. Emergency vehicles in the middle of the road. It was a car crash. The lights from the ambulance and police cars were flickering in the moonlit puddles on the ground. It was a teenager, a young man. He was so sorry. He was driving too fast in the rain. He lost control.

A hand shot up. She had tears in her eyes, "That's my nephew."

I continued to describe everything I saw.

"Oh my God," my friend said. "How do you know that? I've never talked to you about this before." She turned to my other friends as if to defend herself. "I swear to God; we have never talked about this before."

My friend Kristin handed her some tissues.

"Thank you," I said to her nephew.

Next there was a man. He was a father. He was lying in a hospital bed, his head turned to the side to look at his daughter. She was holding his hand and crying.

He was strong and reassuring even though he was the one who was dying. He made a promise to her. "I will still be with you," he said, "I will go to every single game." He showed me himself on the sidelines of soccer games and football games sitting in a lawn chair cheering.

Another friend rose her hand, her voice cracking as she spoke. "That's my dad. That's exactly what he promised me when he was dying." I've always wondered if he was at the games. He loved to support my boys. He came to every game before he got sick.

"Thank you," I said to her dad. "We've got you," he replied. "Don't forget it. We will always show up. Don't forget to ask."

"Thank you," I said to my friends. I bowed to them. "You may now eat your cupcakes!"

I was exhausted but also relieved. I hadn't expected it to be that hard but even when it was hard, Spirit came through. I drove myself to the beach to sit under the stars by myself to take it all in.

Imagine developing your most sacred skill live, in public, with no script and no guarantee anyone will show up—from this world or the next. This is what it takes to be a platform medium.

If I were a singer, I could rehearse a song until I knew it backwards and forwards, sideways and upside down. I could sing alone, sing to friends, sing in secret. But mediumship doesn't work like that. The only way to develop the ability to hold connection after connection for an audience... is to *do it*. Live. In front of strangers. There's no preparation, just guts and grit.

I don't know of any other skill that has to be developed on the fly, in such deep surrender, with so much uncertainty.

And yet, I wasn't letting that slow me down.

Because this work is *that* important. *That* healing. *That* transformative. And I won't let fear of failure stop me.

I didn't have a lot, but one thing I knew I had was courage and resilience. And if I was really going to pursue this and do it for more and more people like I wanted to, that courage was exactly what I needed.

Chapter Fifty-Two

The Divine Feminine

This wasn't easy but it was worth it. If I took a chance on myself and ignored any possible embarrassment or threat of failure, I ended up reaching a new level and that felt really good. At times, I struggled with self-doubt. I was hard on myself, but after my initial reaction passed, I would take some time in meditation and ask what I was meant to learn from the experience. I was beginning to see that failure really was just a mindset that could be ignored.

I started recording the messages for myself in the Voice Notes app on my phone. When I gave a reading, I'd enter the lightly altered consciousness that was that dreamy state that fluttered away quickly when I came back to full consciousness. Recording the messages preserved them so I could go back to them later.

Every time, the messages were so reassuring and positive.

I would ask something like "Why did I do so badly?" and they would immediately reframe my question. "You didn't do badly; you took a chance! Look at what happened! You stretched yourself! You shared something powerful!" My guides never wanted me to look at the one person who left unchanged. They only wanted me to focus on the one person who left completely changed.

One thing that still continued to nag at me was the inner conflict that what I was doing might be seen as wrong in the eyes of God. Sometimes, when I posted my events on Facebook, the comment thread filled with angry reproaches from locals that the moderator should take my post down and that anyone who attends would be risking their soul. They'd quote the bible and call me names. I never posted but others would and a few times, the drama that stirred up caused the post to be removed and even though I never engaged with the comments, I was banned from the group.

Some friends had also distanced themselves from me or even blocked me. They accused me of rejecting God. I understood where they were coming from because I had once believed the same thing, but from my perspective, experiencing everything I had gone through and feeling the pure peace and love of my awakening had only strengthened my belief in God. I was seeing God everywhere in everyone. My faith hadn't waned—it had become more expansive, inclusive, and profound.

I knew I could never convince them and didn't dare to try. In fact, I knew their warnings came from love and protection. If they didn't care, they wouldn't try to protect me. But my perspective had shifted so dramatically because of what I had experienced. There was no way to describe it. It was pointless to defend it. I knew this because I had been in their shoes and I couldn't imagine anything anyone could have said to convince me. I had to experience it.

I felt so lucky to have had the experience of the dream and the man on the couch. It was as if they lifted me from a confused wilderness and carried me back to a place of clarity and recognition. When the man reached into my energy field to take away limiting beliefs and anxieties, he freed me from the worst parts of myself.

"I'm hardly the person who should be picked out of a line up by God to be given a miracle, sudden awakening," I told Jae. I'd been thinking about this almost constantly and the flood of gratitude made me weepy. I'd been saved by chance, by a deceased wife trying to talk to her husband and a disembodied group of guides with sage wisdom and witty takes.

"I disagree," she said. "You're exactly the person."

I continued without listening to her, "I mean, I shit my pants in a Wendy's parking lot. I've never had a healthy relationship. I can't even find my car at the mall without needing to set off the alarm."

She laughed. "Maybe you don't need to be perfect to have a divine awakening. Maybe the fucked-up ones need it most!"

"We really do," I said.

"I'm still waiting for mine!"

"I wish I had a magic wand!" I told her. Since my awakening, I felt different, I was different, but Jae was still struggling. She read all the self-help books. She did the exercises. She had all the wisdom and still that feeling of freedom and the fruits of it in her life eluded her. It wasn't fair. I wanted us to be on this journey together. I wanted her to feel as good as I did. I often felt she deserved it more than I did.

"His power is made perfect in weakness," Jae said. "You've been going through it. I've watched you shrink. You kept adjusting to a life that continued to offer you less. But you're not small. You were just squeezed."

Despite her own struggles, she still showed up to celebrate and encourage me.

"His power is made perfect in weakness," I repeated, "but the bible also says, don't consult psychics or mediums. Which part is right?"

"The good part," she said. "The part where God is love and where we are forgiven. Not the part where we are constantly punished. How can God be love and also jealous and full of wrath? That's not love, that's control and manipulation."

"That's exactly how I'm feeling too. I've been thinking about how the bible was channeled, right? Through humans. When I'm getting evidence and messages, am I channeling? When I'm getting insights from my guides, is it channeling? I think so. I mean, that makes sense to me. So if what these humans were doing is the same as what I'm doing then there's this filter of their own personal story that everything has to go through, right? And if they don't have the word for it, or the image for it, they're going to mangle it. I do it too. That's why you hear that sometimes you aren't the "right medium" for a sitter, because you may not have the exact image or word or experience in your own personal library that you can pull from that will make the message stick."

"I get that," she was listening intently.

"And we are all shaped by our stories and perceptions and even by the time we live in. And in those times, they were violent and marked by fear and control. So their filter would default to fear and control even violence even if the message was more subtle and about self-punishment. I don't know if I'm making sense."

"You're making sense," she confirmed.

"And I think about how much has changed. If someone says to us now that we can talk to people and see the face of someone across the planet while we are talking, that's no big deal, but if someone said that a hundred years ago it would seem like science fiction and even terrifying."

"Right."

"We are experiencing things differently. If the bible was channeled now, it would have different filters. Maybe our new filters would get just as much wrong but we would get different things wrong and then someone in 400 years would correct that to." I was getting heated, I took a breath. "So, I just trust my inner knowing. Anything that the bible says that is good, loving and healing, that part is right. And the parts that are full of threats? I ignore it. I dismiss it as a product of another time that no longer applies. That was the pre – enlightenment era, pre-cell phone era."

"You're right," she said. "And also I disagree. I mean, I can't speak to the channeling. That sounds right and I trust your interpretation of it from your experience. But there's more here. The bible was heavily edited. There are books that were never printed. Even within the books there are discrepancies. The discrepancies may come from the filter, like you said, but I think they were intentionally edited to suppress and control people, to make them dependent on the systems of power. God is in us. We don't need an interpreter, but as soon as we claim that and know it? We become a threat."

"Amen, sister!" I shouted. We were both getting heated.

Her eyes flashed. "A man has a vision, and it's divine revelation. A woman has one, and she's a witch."

"Preach!"

"A man channels God, they put robes on him. A woman does, and they burn her. They don't fear our intuition because it is evil. They fear it because it is real. Women's intuition isn't superstition, it's a direct line to wisdom that bypasses their authority. No wonder they spent centuries convincing us to doubt the very thing that gave us strength."

This was resonating with me so strongly. All my struggles with self-doubt had been instilled in me by systems or people that benefited from my lack of confidence which manifested as a lack of will. This wasn't just about me learning to trust the nudges but all of us. Everyone who dares to reclaim intuition, man or woman, threatens the foundations of systems built on our self-doubt. Every time we trust ourselves instead of seeking external validation or permission, we're dismantling centuries of control.

Chapter Fifty-Three

Getting Personal

"I want a reading," my daughter said. "Can you give me a reading?"

I was visiting my daughter at college. Her father and stepmother helped her move into the dorms and the next week, I went up to help with loose ends. We made Target runs for bathroom caddies, a trip to Best Buy for phone chargers. Then, just like any other female college freshman, she needed an emergency trip to Lululemon for leggings. It was so good to see her happy.

"Just one pair," I said, giving in happily. I'd given a 30-minute reading to a friend of a friend on zoom, and she'd sent me a hundred dollars.

I was expecting her request for leggings, but I was not expecting her request for a reading.

Right at the beginning of the Covid lockdowns, her best friend Audrey's older sister took her own life. It was a shock to everyone. I knew that was who she wanted to reach.

"Of course," I said. "Whenever you're ready."

"I'm ready right now," she said.

We were having lunch at a restaurant in an outdoor mall in Raleigh. There were people at the tables near us, a lot of distractions. It was a different environment from the protected one I was used to. I didn't want to disappoint her, but just as importantly, I wanted to push myself to see if I could give a quality reading in less-than-ideal circumstances. But looking at my daughter's eyes, this was important.

I agreed. "Alright," I said. "Can I have your consent to connect with your loved ones in spirit for the highest good?"

"Yes."

She looked at me intently. I looked to the side, over her shoulder but was looking inward. What did my body feel like, what messages, impressions, emotions were emerging within me as evidence.

Then I felt my uncle saying, "Who do you think it is?" My grandmother was there too. I chuckled. "It's grandmama and uncle Hooty," I said.

"Oh, what do they have to say?"

I tried to feel in for evidence. How do I get evidence for my uncle and grandmother to give to my daughter? I knew them so well and so, did she? How would I come up with something undeniable that there was no way I'd know. It wasn't possible!

"Get to the point!" my uncle said warmly. So, I started right in on the message. My daughter didn't need the evidence. She already knew. She trusted me. That's when I learned that not everyone is going to require evidence, just like not everyone will want a message. For some people, there will be nothing you do that is wrong. And for other people nothing you do will be right.

"Uncle Hooty is saying that you don't have to make everything so hard for it to be important. Take some light classes."

"Woah," my daughter said. "I was thinking about that just this morning!"

I hadn't known that. She and I hadn't talked about her classes, just about her supplies. The message was evidence enough for my daughter. She wanted more.

I gave her as much as I could and then I felt their energy walk away.

"I think that's it," I said.

"Is there anyone else?" I felt into it. "Yes," I said. "There's a young woman. I think it might be Audrey's sister."

"What is she saying?"

I wanted to give her evidence for the sister. I'd never met her and didn't know much about her. I only knew the circumstances of her passing.

I shared the evidence I was getting, about her personality, the things she liked to do, the way she looked. She was accomplished and admired. She was popular.

"Yes! That's her!" my daughter said, with excitement. Then as if she couldn't hold back her eagerness she leaned over the table toward me. "Ask her if it was her in my dream."

"Of course it was," Audrey answered. I had no idea about any dream. My mediumistic mind and my motherly mind were both trying to work at once.

"Of course it was," I repeated for my daughter. "She is saying, 'yes, it was her.'"

"Why?" my daughter asked. "Why would she be in *my* dream and not in Audrey's?"

My daughter had tears in her eyes. Her best friend had been struggling ever since her sister's death. The entire family was reeling from it. Her parents had lost their jobs, moved away. Her best friend had retreated.

"Audrey needs her!" she said through tears.

The sister replied solemnly. "Audrey's grief was too deep for her to be reached. She was in a pit of grief."

I had a flash of the moment I woke up from the nap in James' bed. The pit of despair. Audrey was in the pit of despair. The sister showed herself holding onto Audrey while she cried, but Audrey didn't know she was there.

"She's constantly with Audrey but her grief is too deep and it's hard for her to be reached. She knew you were her best friend, so she came to you so you could tell her she was okay."

My daughter was crying and nodding. It all made sense to her.

Tears welled up in my eyes too. My heart sank under the awareness that even the young people are suffering with grief this heavy. Young beautiful girls full of hope and promise, like Audrey, were in the pit of despair from grief. And young beautiful girls like her sister had found the suffering to be too much.

If giving readings could help pull someone up out of that pit, even just closer to the top so the grief wasn't as heavy, so they had a fighting chance to get out, then every bit of suffering I experienced that brought me to this place where I could be a medium was worth it.

Chapter Fifty-Four

On Stage, On Purpose

I was obsessed with giving readings. The sense of fulfillment at having provided something of value to someone was immense. In addition, I was still
not sure any of this was real. If I wasn't in the midst of a reading, it was hard to
believe what was happening.

The more times I gave a reading, and the sitter could validate the evidence, the
more I would believe mediumship was real. Practicing one on one wasn't enough.
I wanted to put myself in tougher situations with more distractions, more energy,
more pressure. I wanted my readings to sparkle like diamonds. I wanted to make
a difference.

I was feeling burnt out. I was doing too much. I was taking classes, raising kids,
working long hours on weekdays and trying to give as many readings as I could.
I needed to take a break but when I mentioned feeling over-committed, everyone
suggested I drop the mediumship. It was so unfair. I was working so hard and the
only thing I could eliminate to ease my stress was the only thing that brought me
any joy.

I was learning how to trust the evidence, giving exactly what was given from
spirit no matter how unusual it seemed.

At one demonstration, I was bringing through a middle-aged man who kept
showing me a parking lot. I knew that there's always more than what you think
you are seeing but spirit doesn't waste a thought, so I had to go with it.

"This is random" I said. "But I've got to say it. I keep seeing a parking lot."

I went deeper. What kind of parking lot? What was the feeling around this parking lot? Any other associations with this parking lot.

"This feels like the parking lot to a family restaurant. I see a wheelchair access ramp made from cement. It feels nicer than fast food but still very informal. I see a big plastic menu with the corners starting to peel. I see big booths with red plasticky leather seats. The restaurant I'm seeing feels like one you'd go to on a road trip or after a soccer game.

It feels both celebratory and routine, like you'd gone there regularly but for special events. He feels like he's here for his daughter and he's wanting to say how proud he is. He's seen your achievements and he's so proud."

I'd shared everything I could pull out of this parking lot and was still doubting if I'd gotten into my imagination or was really bringing through a link.

"Can anyone take this evidence? I know it's random, but that's what I was getting."

I was convinced no hands would go up. But then one did.

"I can take it," a woman in the third row said. "That's my dad. He passed when I was five. I only have two memories of him because I was so young. All my other memories were formed from things people told me about him, but I have two memories of my own and one of them was going to this family restaurant together."

The room went quiet. This was the kind of moment you can't predict or plan. It is impossible to walk away and be unchanged. It wasn't just the right evidence. It was the only evidence. She had so few memories to work from. But this one landed. It was also an important reminder to me to share whatever spirit was giving me. Spirit doesn't waste a thought, doesn't waste an image. Spirit knows what evidence will resonate. It's not my job to interpret, rate or qualify the evidence. It's my job to deliver it.

There's no room for my doubts, my fears, my second guessing or even protecting myself from embarassment. I need to leave all those at the door when I show up to speak for spirit. I am there to do a job and the biggest part of it is getting out of the way. This wasn't about me. This was bigger than me. Then, like a spark in my mind, the question I'd wrestled with was answered. "Why me?" Because I have courage.

Chapter Fifty-Five

Pushing Boundaries

I loved a challenge. Not just any challenge but a challenge that felt worthwhile. Everything with mediumship felt worthwhile. It felt necessary. If I was going to do it, I was going to overdo it. I was going to go all in.

One of the benefits of being single was that there was no one who could stop me from chasing every squirrel.

If this was real, and I was able to do it, why wouldn't I try to do it at the highest level to bring the most comfort? Not just grandmothers winking and pinching cheeks with "I love you's." Not just fathers saying, "I'm so proud," or "I'm sorry." Not that those weren't important, they were. But what could I do to really stretch the limits and use this gift to serve those who were desperately in need, not just curious?

I'd asked a friend if she knew anyone in law enforcement who might be open to using a medium. She connected me with a private investigator she'd known for years. She said she didn't know much about how he worked but it was worth a shot.

I reached out to him, and he confided that he had used mediums before many times. He said the mediums he'd worked with before all had their own way of working and asked if I used pictures, if I did the work from a distance or if I had any preferences.

I told him I was brand new and wasn't sure what my style was but that I was wanting to explore my abilities to see if I could be of service. He said he had a case that he could take me to as a test case so I could explore if this kind of work was what I really wanted to do, and he could validate if the kind of information I got was going to be useful him. It was already a closed case but he had more information than the general public and so he would be able to confirm if the information I got was accurate.

I told Jae about my plans before I left. "Are you nervous?" she asked. "I would be freaked out."

"Not really."

"What if you are talking to a violent criminal? A bad person on the other side? It could give you nightmares."

"I'm not worried about that," I said. "I'm a little nervous about the detective though. I've never met him before. I trust spirit more than people."

"Good point," she said. We were both getting a little worked up.

"I'm far more scared of people than spirits."

"People are the worst."

"They are!"

As I drove to see Ralph, I called upon my angels, inviting them to be with me. I'd never done this before, but I was listening to a lot of podcasts and heard other mediums and psychics talk about this. They said, "Your angels are always with you. Spirit is always with you! The universe is grateful when you take on this work to heal hearts and open minds!"

I believed everything I wanted to believe and nothing I didn't. That was my new way of being. I was living my life with radical delusion. Fueling my dreams with wild conviction. There is no failure, only growth! I resist repression and live in full expression!

It was a two-lane road with trees on each side. I had to slow down to cross a railroad track. I tried to settle into that receptive state.

As I waited for my angels to show up, I wondered if I would feel them or see them. Was it even safe to do this while driving? And who would it be? I was feeling brave going to a crime scene. Even if it was just a practice scene, it held a different kind of significance in my mind that this work could lead to one day connecting with the victim of a crime to bring closure to a family and justice. Maybe Jesus himself would show up. Jesus was a big deal and this was a big deal.

Right at that thought, I felt the energy shift. My car felt fully occupied. Not only were there several in the car but they were all leaning forward, watching the road. I guess there's no need for seatbelts. One of them was leaning right between the front seats and I felt his face almost touching mine, watching the road with me.

"I pity the fool!" Mr. T said and I felt his hands on my shoulders, pumping me up.

It wasn't Jesus or an Archangel. It was the cast of a canceled 80's TV show. It was the A Team! But as I laughed, I trusted it was exactly who I needed.

"That's right!" I thought. I pity the fool who thinks he can get away with a crime when I'm on the case!

Spirit never wastes a thought and especially when something comes from out of nowhere, it's meaningful.

The meaning was clear. We get exactly what we need in the moment, whether we realize or accept it or not. My psyche got just who I needed, and I was here for it! Because while this was important, sacred work, it's also life, and life should be fun. Taking on a challenge should be fun. Always look at what opportunities for growth can come when we challenge ourselves.

So, there I was, driving my three-cylinder manual shift Mirage, low gas, low pressure in a tire but somehow hanging on to take me to a crime scene across town with Mr. T and the gang in the back. "I love it when a plan comes together," I heard, and couldn't help but smile.

I pulled into the lot and saw a man standing by a motorcycle. He started to approach me as I got out of my car.

After the necessary introductions, I looked at his bike and said, "Are we going together? My car? Or how about your bike?"

"Up to you," he said.

"Bike," I said.

He handed me a helmet and I hopped on behind him. Only when we were a mile up the road, crossing a small bridge did it occur to me that I had just gotten on the back of a motorcycle with a complete stranger to drive to an undisclosed place. I really hoped the violent death I was about to explore wasn't my own.

It was cool out. The weather had just turned from hot and humid to cool and crisp in the last week. The leaves were starting to turn, and a few had fallen and started to collect on the sides of the road. As we crossed another bridge, I started to feel nauseous. We must be close.

Ralph angled his bike to the right and we turned onto a gravel driveway to a small park. There were picnic benches under a shelter and a cement building. He parked and we both got off the bike. He said I should walk around and see what I could get.

As had become my routine, before I felt into the energy, I said a prayer.

"Christ, protect me from all forms of self-doubt. Give me a clear line of communication with a helpful spirit to share evidence that will lead to resolution, healing and closure for the highest good. Protect me from all low vibrational energy that doesn't serve the highest good or the healing intention of this reading. Use my senses in a way to help, sharing only what is necessary and nothing more."

As I was walking down a path past the picnic benches toward the water, I felt a sharp pinch in the back left of my head.

"I've got someone with me," I said trying not to think about how weird I must sound. "It's a man, a young man, in his twenties, I think. I've got pain in the back of my head and a constriction in my throat. And vomit."

"Yes," he said. "That's right."

The excitement and nerves of the moment pulled me out of the moment. I walked around hoping to feel the connection again, but I didn't feel like anyone was with me anymore. It was just me and my nerves.

I struggled to get more than that. I felt stuck.

"I'm not getting much more," I finally admitted. "I'm usually very visual but I'm not seeing anything."

"Makes sense," he said.

"It does?"

"Yes." He elaborated. "I heard you praying. You prayed for protection and only to see what you needed. That was a smart move. This scene was gruesome. You wouldn't want to see that."

"No, I wouldn't," I agreed.

"I'll give you some information to work with," he said. "It was a young man, in his twenties. Cause of death was trauma to the head. Can you tell me more about the object? Can you tell me who else was there?"

And then I saw him. He was thin with light brown, dark blond hair and smooth skin.

"He's older than he looks," I said. "He's got a babyface."

"Yes."

"He was in the military, and he was coming here to meet someone he knew but didn't know long. I think it was a date, but she isn't the one who hurt him, there was someone else."

"Yes, how many?"

"I'm just seeing her and one other. She came from over here," I pointed toward where we parked. "And someone else came from over there." I pointed to a small building. "They may have met online, possibly a date. He was excited to come here. I feel anticipation. He was looking for a good time. He wanted to party. He'd been drinking. He's showing me it was nighttime, and he was already buzzed because his eyes weren't adjusting well to the lights against the dark sky, and he was feeling like time was going very quickly and his senses felt heightened. He was having a good time and then suddenly there's a sharp change in the mood. Something unexpected. Someone is threatening him and he's trying to negotiate. He's pleading with them."

"Yes, you're getting it," he said.

"And while he was trying to de-escalate, he was hit hard in the back of the head from behind. He didn't see it coming."

"Was the pain from impact or a gunshot," he asked.

"I haven't done a reading with a gunshot before," I said, "but I did one recently where the man was kicked hard in the back of the head, and it felt like that. Felt like a hard object striking the head. Not a gunshot."

"Correct," he said. "Anything else? Can you tell me how many people were there?"

I tried to lean into it. "I can't tell," I said.

"Not a problem," he said. "Anything else?"

"He's showing me a man again. A middle-aged man with a pointy beard. It comes to a point at the chin. And he's thin and not too tall."

Ralph nodded. "You did great."

I felt satisfied. I wouldn't say excited because it was somber and heavy, but I knew I did good work.

"Can I show you a picture?" he asked.

"I really don't want to see," I said.

"Not the victim. Not the scene." He was scrolling through his phone. "It's the man you just described. The man who killed him. With the pointy beard. I have a photo of him in court."

He pulled up a picture of the suspect wearing a prison jumpsuit with his hands in cuffs being led into the courtroom. You could see he had a goatee with a sharp point at the chin. "There's the beard just as you described it. How you were touching your face and chin, that's it."

He was right, as I was talking, I had been drawing the beard on my own face into a little point, like I was stroking the hair into shape.

Next, he showed me the victim. He was young and handsome with startlingly blue aquamarine eyes and a soft baby face.

"Thank you," I said. "Thank you for letting me do this."

"You did great," he said. "Any time you want to do this again; I've got a lot of cold cases that could use something special. We've done all we can with our own faculties, and you've definitely got a gift."

As I followed him to the bike, I noticed I felt dizzy. I must have been more deeply connected than I realized. I steadied myself and kept walking. We went back to the parking lot, I got his card and gave him mine, we shook hands and had initiated something important.

Driving home I realized how much adrenaline I still had going through me. I made a mental note to remember how the spirit only spoke to me through clairsentience at the beginning because it was protecting me from the gruesome visuals. And when the victim did give me visuals, they weren't graphic. The victim's photo looked like a school picture. The perpetrator's looked like a mugshot.

I wanted to do it again. This was somewhere my abilities could make a dramatic difference; not just in comforting the living with memories of their loved ones, but in giving voice to those who could no longer speak for themselves. I felt like I was doing something that truly mattered.

Chapter Fifty-Six

The Christ in Me

The last time I went home to Pittsburgh, I had reconnected with a friend from my childhood. I was staying in my parents' house while they were traveling, and the grass had grown ankle high. I'd mowed the lawn but needed someone to haul away the grass and leaves. My mom told me David had a lawn care business, so I called him. She was still friends with his mother, so I reached out right away. As it turned out, he had closed his business but would still find someone to help me.

I had reached the point where I knew I was committing to the mediumship path with wild conviction and had decided to speak about it openly. I was stepping into confidence, claiming my feminine birthright and taking charge of my life with radical delusion.

The act of announcing it helped me claim it. It motivated me to take it on with confidence, even though I was still struggling with some self-doubt. I'd also lost some friendships, a pattern I'd experienced several times in my life due to divorce, break-ups, and moves, where I found out who was really a friend and who was just going through the motions. I knew I needed true friends, so there was even some intentionality about my boldness. If a friend was going to leave, then leave now.

Then, we got to catching up. I told him I had recently discovered I was able to communicate with the dead and was doing it intentionally, he reacted without any surprise. "Very good," he'd said, with immediate, unfiltered encouragement.

"That doesn't surprise me at all about you. There has always been something different about you."

I was taken aback.

He went on to share that he had his own abilities. He knew when people would call or show up. He could feel their presence in advance. It wasn't the same kind of sensitivity as mine, but like I was learning, he had come to realize it was a gift and something he could use to make his life more manageable if he listened to the nudges instead of ignoring them.

He also was able to gain inexplicable insights in quiet moments that transcended explanation. For me, they happened while driving, folding laundry, or doing dishes. For him, they happened in nature. There were certain places he could go where the trees would whisper, the water would ripple, and clear insights would pour into his awareness with a sense of calm and completion that I understood without him having to find the words.

We'd experienced similar setbacks and disappointments that gave us another common ground. Despite growing up with some financial privilege, we both found ourselves barely scraping by. We were both pushing through a time in our lives when we felt like life was all work and no play. All effort and no reward. It's very hard and frankly unpleasant to try to explain to someone how hard life can feel when you can't afford groceries, when you can't figure out why your efforts are coming up short. You know people suspect you aren't trying hard enough, are being dramatic or have somehow brought this on yourself. It doesn't make sense, especially from their experience where there is more flow.

We didn't have to explain our struggles to each other, we recognized it in the subtext. No defending or explaining necessary. We "got it," and did what people do when we see our suffering worn on someone else: we immediately volunteered to be a support and encouragement. We knew that's all the other needed. We knew how to do it, we did it all the time for others.

Despite talking almost daily, I still hadn't seen him in decades. So, the next time I went to town, I was looking forward to catching up in person.

The night I arrived in Pittsburgh, he texted to say that he had come down with something bad, a terrible flu, maybe even Covid, and wouldn't be able to see me because he was too sick.

The timing for him to get sick was terrible. He had just moved into a new apartment the day before and hadn't even filled the fridge. He was in launch mode for a new business that was physically and mentally demanding. I knew immediately that this wasn't just an illness, this was a crisis. There are no days off when you are in survival mode.

So, the next morning, I woke up at 5:30 so I could get to the grocery store when it opened at 6 am. I bought chicken noodle soup, yogurt, NyQuil, Dayquil, and several prepared meals as well as a box of tea and a jar of honey. As a single person, when you are sick, it isn't even just the down time that gets you, but also the logistics of caring for yourself. There's no one to go to the store, no one to make the food. No one catch the balls you're juggling before they fall. Right when you need to take care of your person the most, you are forced to abandon yourself. It's not a priority.

I was short on cash but knew that spending $100 on food would not break me. It had kept me up late and woken me early. I felt compelled to go to the store. It was the same irrefutable urging that had compelled me to send the text messages, with the same intensity that compelled me to share deeply personal messages from spirit.

At the same time, I found myself overthinking. I had a bad history with men. I'd been accused of mothering, and smothering. I did too much, too soon. Was I trying to earn his friendship? Was I trying to earn love? I wanted to hold myself accountable. I had come too far to fall back into self-destructive behavior.

These thoughts played in my mind while I drove to his house at sunrise. I had a bag full of groceries in the passenger seat next to me, with everything healthy I could think of. Bone broth, vitamins, tissues. Exactly what I would have bought if he were my child, or my parent. Exactly what I would want to have on hand if it were me.

He had no idea I'd been to the store and bought these things. If I was being "too much" I could still just turn back to my parents' house and put them in the fridge there. Was I being "too much?"

Then, I heard the phrase clear and strong in my mind. There was no doubt.

"This is the Christ in me."

The words came through with such clarity that I almost looked to see if someone else was in the car. This wasn't just a thought—it was a presence, a knowing that filled the space around me as I drove down the familiar streets of my hometown. The morning light was just breaking over the buildings, and in that ordinary moment, something extraordinary was unfolding. My eyes started to water. I felt the undeniable presence of pure love.

"This is the Christ in me," came again, just as clear.

The revelation wasn't accompanied by burning bushes or choirs of angels, just the hum of tires on asphalt and the smell of roast chicken from the grocery bag. Yet it was profound in its simplicity. In that most ordinary of spaces, the driver's seat of my car, I was receiving divine wisdom that cut through all my doubts and second-guessing.

At that moment, all my hesitation vanished. My heart slowed and my breath got deeper. I sent him a text saying I had some food to drop off and could he let me in when I got there. He was already awake, having not slept at all, and responded quickly.

This is the Christ in me. It's the Christ in all of us to help in whatever ways that we are able, to show up for each other. To love each other without any expectation of reciprocation just as we would hope to love ourselves. "Do unto others" in action.

Some people travel to ashrams in India or hike the Camino de Santiago searching for spiritual revelations. Some pay for expensive retreats in Sedona. Some explore plant medicine and hypnosis. But here I was, finding profound truth while driving to drop off soup for a sick friend. The sacred doesn't always announce itself with fanfare. Sometimes it whispers to us in traffic, or while we're washing dishes, or when we're hesitating between selfishness and generosity.

The car had become my sanctuary more than once now. First the A-Team spirit guides cheering me on, and now this deeper message about the divine within. The feminine desire to nurture and protect rose up in me like a calling. Perhaps there was something about the liminal space of driving, alone with my thoughts yet in motion that made it easier to hear the whispers of spirit. Or maybe it was simply that God speaks to us wherever we are, no matter what we are doing and we only need to be open enough to hear it.

I realized that all the spiritual growth I'd been experiencing wasn't leading me away from ordinary life but deeper into it. I was finding the extraordinary within the everyday. The Christ consciousness wasn't something distant or separate, but a living force within me, within all of us, activated in those moments when we choose love over fear, generosity over self-protection.

As I pulled up to his apartment building, I knew that this moment of clarity was a gift. The groceries weren't about him or me anymore. They were about honoring the divine spark that had guided me here, the Christ in me reaching out to the Christ in him, in an ordinary act of kindness on an ordinary morning when I had plenty to share.

Chapter Fifty-Seven

Manifesting

I was back in school. I was just over halfway through the MBA program and had to keep up to make sure I finished before time ran out. My son was applying to schools this time. I woke up early to make breakfast, logged in early to keep up with work and as soon as the business day was over, I logged into school, reading chapters, listening to lectures, taking quizzes. At the peak of my exhaustion, I read my son's essays and tried to have conversations about his life.

It was too much. I was tired. I needed some relief. One day, I sat in my bed and did a manifestation meditation. I enjoyed meditating when I had a chance to do it. I found I could quickly move to that luminous space where my forehead and crown would tingle letting me know my third eye was open. Even twenty minutes in this space was rejuvenating.

I listened to a guided meditation on attracting abundance with ease. Reject the thoughts that tell you that abundance comes from work, effort and earning, the voice said. Repeat these words, "I am a magnet for abundance. I attract abundance with ease in familiar and surprising ways."

The guide encouraged us to visualize what it would feel like to have the abundance we were seeking. She said to write down what we wanted.

I wanted financial security. I wanted to have so much money I didn't have to think about it. Not that I needed to be wealthy in an exorbitant way, but if I needed tires for my car, I just wanted to replace them, without the panic, without the frantic search for ways to bridge the gap. Maybe it meant having enough money that someone could help me manage it. I needed to get on track for retirement. People in my family tended to live a very long time. I needed to support myself. As funny as the plan to live in a tent full of chickens in my son's back yard was, it wasn't what I really wanted. I wanted autonomy, healthy food, a secure roof, company, and my God I wanted to get out of the house and do a couple things, go a couple places before I die!

I wrote it down.

Then the voice said to make it even bigger. Make the dream wildly bigger.

I followed the instructions. I wrote down that I wanted so much money that I could be a source of abundance and security for the people I loved. My children, my parents, my friends. I wanted to have more than enough money to help support their dreams, to provide a safety net when things got tough, to be someone they could count on. I didn't want any of us to panic at a bill. In my mind this felt like tens of thousands of dollars in the bank. The kind of money you don't have to check when you need new tires. You just swipe and you still get to eat.

The meditation ended. I felt refreshed and energized and I got back to work. It was hard to believe that manifestation could work. That visualizing a potential future and leaning into what it felt like would be enough to create meaningful change. I wasn't here to analyze things anymore. I was here to live with wild, unbridled conviction. To be free. I could believe anything. And if anything was worth believing in, it was me.

Chapter Fifty-Eight

What if I Lose My Connection?

I 'd been giving readings for over two years. I'd been promoted to a professional medium on VerySoul. I gave readings at Alchemy & Aura, the same store I went to for support, in the very same room I received my reading, I was now working on Saturdays from 11-5. On top of that I was hosting platform mediumship events every month at Belle Vue Wilmington for groups of ten to twenty participants.

My life was different in many ways, but also the same. I was far less anxious but still struggled with doubt at times. I hadn't eliminated my stress, but I was handling it better. I was still struggling financially but the income from readings was giving me space to breathe.

My confidence in private readings was strong, but I wanted to get better at demonstrations. There is so much stigma around mediumship. Hosting demonstrations gave people an opportunity to experience a mediumship event without committing to a private session. They could see how a reading unfolded without having to invest fully.

I also liked the fact that a demonstration was a place where skeptics might show up. A woman with strong intuition who felt her own connection to spirit might bring her husband to a demonstration. I saw myself in him: the skepticism, guarded, afraid of being taken advantage of. But things happen in a demonstration, whether the reading is for you or someone else that just can't be explained any other way than admitting there must be something more. What more means might be different for all of us: God, the universe, spirit, the quantum field. It expands our minds and hearts in a way that invites possibility, and possibility is a gateway to healing. So many of us feel stuck, alone and unvalued. The possibility there's something more to work with than the tools you've already exhausted, the thought that you aren't alone, you are surrounded by love and support, and you are valued, cherished and the love you thought you lost is still with you.

All it took for me was an experience with something I couldn't explain any other way than to open my mind to the possibility there was more than I could explain or even understand. And from that, I got so much healing. If I can be part of the moment that challenges the beliefs that hold us back so someone can find their way to a new possibility, I've performed an everyday miracle. It's the Christ in me.

Chapter Fifty-Nine

The Big Event

D espite all the success I'd been having, there still was a quiet fear that this connection to spirit was temporary, conditional, and just waiting for the right moment to disappear.

I recognized the pattern in multiple relationships and even jobs, I'd feel seen, supported, valued and that would lead me to let my guard down, give without condition, sacrifice and bend, only to realize too late, that the promise was a lie. There was no reciprocation. I'd emptied myself and there was barely a drop left to sustain me. I'd played the fool so many times. I couldn't take that freefall again. It would break me.

I wondered if the love I felt from the spirit world would follow the same script. The gradual buildup of trust, the wonderful peak of connection, followed by the inevitable crash. Was mediumship just another version of this story, but with spirits instead of men? Would the other side, too, eventually abandon me once I put myself out there completely?

I'd invited everyone I knew to my next demonstration. It would be my biggest and boldest yet! I'd been giving demonstrations to a handful of friends at an intimate event space close to my house, but this event was different. I rented a room at a gorgeous event space called Belle Vue in the Brooklyn Arts District of Wilmington, NC. I posted tickets for sale on social media, sharing them in community pages, my personal page and even paying $30 to boost the event. The room was packed. There were friends in the audience, and strangers. My friend

Kelley, who I'd given my first donated reading to on VerySoul drove from Western North Carolina to attend. It was my big debut! Everything was falling into place.

While I was pleased with my development, I also knew that when I was back in school, mediumship would be on hold. It was too much to do both with school. I had to give myself a break.

Standing in the wings before the event, I was overcome with the energy. It was hard to tell the difference between the dense bubbles of spirit coming close to share my energetic body and the crispy noise of anxiety in my nervous system. Everything was running on all cylinders.

I wasn't worried about the public speaking aspect. I was afraid of being exposed as a fraud, not because I was deceiving anyone, but because what if I was deceiving myself? What if this wasn't even real and I'd been fooled by my own mind, by my friends, by everyone who'd claimed I was making a genuine connection for them. What if the voice in my head that whispered there was something wrong with me for most of my life was the one that was right. What if it wasn't radical delusion but systemic deception?

I had to steady myself. The truth was that every time I stepped onto the platform or opened the zoom or sat with someone, spirit came forward with love and doubt faded into background. This time would be no different, I reminded myself. The evidence would come through, specific details I couldn't possibly have known, validated immediately by audience members with tears of joy and relief in their eyes.

I wasn't going to let the self-doubt that kept me small at work and in my relationships keep me small with spirit.

"I am a clear channel. I serve spirit for the highest good." I said my affirmations loudly before stepping in front of the audience.

Once on stage, the first face I saw was my daughters. She'd driven two hours to come support me. She'd dressed up for the event and looked so professional and grown. I was overwhelmed just looking at the woman she wase becoming.

Every other seat was also filled. There were so many people looking at me. I gave my introduction then asked everyone to take a moment to invite their loved ones close with some deep breaths. In my previous events, everyone closed their eyes with me, took a deep breath and listened to the brief clip of music to give us a moment of intention. But this time, people stood up to go to the bathroom. Others looked at their watches or phones. The room was too hot. It was stagnant. I'd overestimated the comfortable capacity of the room and people were already antsy, fanning themselves with my brochure, looking at their watches.

I thanked everyone for coming and said, "Let's see who is here…" to move into the first connection.

I got a link right away, a young man who had passed in a traffic accident. I wasn't sure immediately who I was with as there was more than one person who could recognize him. I knew I had to get more specific evidence. Something that would make the connection undeniable.

I got a flash of him moving to the right and felt my body pulled to the right like I was looking over my shoulder. I had to share it. Spirit doesn't waste a thought.

"I feel like I'm moving to the right. He was driving. Maybe he was reaching for the radio? Talking to a passenger?"

"No passenger," the woman replied. "He was alone."

Maybe the other woman could connect with this information.

"Does this make sense to you?" I asked.

"No."

I decided to move on. We can't get stuck on a "no" they are part of the process, part of the deepening. This is about quality not perfection.

But the next piece of evidence didn't land. I asked spirit for more. They showed me a room filled with couches with teens lounging. This landed.

"Yes," the first woman said. "He came to my house all the time with his friends. He was close with my son, and they played video games, watched movies, ate pizza. They are such a great group of kids. He is very missed." Then she offered more. "He was driving home at night and was pulling off to exit the highway when he crashed." She paused, then continued, "I guess that's what you were saying, moving to the right. He was on the exit ramp."

You could feel the energy in the room shift. Several people gasped. It was as if we all were sharing a brain, making the same connection to the previous evidence of him moving to the right at the exact same moment. It wasn't exact, but it was correct. That was enough.

After that, I brought through a mother-in-law, a mother, and a son who went by the name Chef and came through with a dog he loved dearly.

Then I brought through an older woman that no one recognized. She talked about being in a nursing home with nurses and staff but her own personal items close by to make her more comfortable. She talked about the music playing in the room and said she could hear it even though she was hard of hearing and thanked her loved one for playing it. The details felt specific. Someone thought they recognized her but there was no music. I moved on. It happens. Sometimes I feel like I have a strong connection, but no one raises their hand. It can feel defeating but it's part of the process. The only thing to do is keep going.

Then I brought through a middle-aged man. I described his way of dressing, his personality, his attitudes about life. Again, crickets. A couple in the front was paying close attention. The woman said, "I think that's him," she was nudging her husband.

"No," he said. Arms folded over his chest. "Too vague."

She agreed but was smiling. "Keep going," she said to me.

I shared more. She nodded and smiled then looked to her husband for validation.

He shook his head. "No," he said. "She could be describing anyone."

I kept trying. I should have moved on, but I wanted to make them happy. I wanted to prove the connection. I wanted to do well. I fell into the mode of earning, reaching, trying and slipped out of the link.

I couldn't get it back. I felt heavy like I was trying to pick up a boulder to look underneath for a tiny pebble of evidence. My body was tense.

I was getting no after no. I wanted to get a clear message. But the more I went on, the more the crowd started to fidget. Someone got up and left.

"Well, it seems like I'm having an off night," I said, not wanting to show the defeat I was feeling. This was so embarrassing. There were so many people. They had paid to come, and I stood in front of them and failed.

After I left the stage, I hid in the back room. The camera man came back to gather his things. "That was awful," I confessed, secretly hoping he'd contradict me.

"It was pretty rough," he agreed. "Happens to the best of them."

I forced myself to go out and mingle fighting back tears. Walking to my car, I felt the familiar weight of shame settle over me. This was different from the private doubts I'd harbored. This was public failure, witnessed by dozens. I'd been exposed as exactly what I feared I might be—someone who couldn't consistently deliver on what she promised, someone who could be accused as "making it up."

I sat in my car, key in the ignition, but didn't start it. The floor had fallen out—my abilities had failed me in the most public way possible. I closed my eyes, not in meditation or seeking guidance, but simply because I couldn't bear to face reality yet.

The next day, I checked in with my higher self. "Why wasn't my connection strong? What did I do wrong?"

The answer came quickly, and just like always it was the positive reframe I needed.

"Your connection was strong, but it wasn't always clear." my guides said. "Your thinking mind was too activated. There was some self-consciousness, ego, and a desire to achieve a specific result. There was a lot of noise in the way. You are trying new things and pushing yourself. This is what happens when you move out of the familiar. It is uncomfortable, there are new things to master. You have learned how to connect and communicate with spirit. Now you need to learn how to handle a room, manage an event. These are all things you can handle but you have to encounter them first to identify what is needed. You are encountering a lot of new things at once. You push yourself farther and as a result you grow faster."

If it's not working, it's teaching.

I called my friend Cindy, a medium I met through VerySoul. We had become fast friends, navigating the world of spirit and work together.

"You did great," she said. "There are going to be hard nights, but you got some links. You didn't force. You were honest with yourself and honored yourself by stopping when it was right to stop. That's it. That's your job. You're not a machine! You're human!"

A couple days later, I got an email. "The woman you were connecting with at the end. I just know that was my mother. I was afraid to interrupt because you were working with the gentleman at the front and I just didn't know, but I haven't been able to stop thinking about it and I knew I had to write you. You described her perfectly. The music that was playing, that was me. I sang to her. The items on her bedside table, I remember them vividly. Thank you so much for your courage in sharing your gift. It was a tough crowd, but your message has really helped me, and I wanted you to know."

That raised a new point. Every missed link wasn't a complete failure. I might have been delivering the right mail to the wrong address. There was so much to learn. I was committed to the journey no matter how bumpy the trip.

Chapter Sixty

Claiming My Life

J ae finally came for a visit. It was the beginning of summer. Like me, she didn't have money for fancy vacations. We escaped our lives by visiting each other's. My kids were at Disney with their dad and stepmom, so their rooms were free for guests.

I worked at my desk while she sat on the porch to read or took her son to activities in town: the sea turtle hospital, the museum, and mini golf. After work, we went to a salt cave to clear our aura then had dinner on the riverfront. One morning before work, we went to sunrise yoga on the pier. Even with still working in the day, it felt like a vacation for me, too. Instead of hiding in my house studying, I was going out to eat and exploring places I wouldn't have gone to alone.

She also came with me to readings at other people's homes. Someone would get a reading; tell a friend and I'd get a call to go to a new house. I was the traveling, after-hours medium.

It struck me how much trust was needed. Sometimes, I wouldn't get anything. Other times, the evidence and messages came through vividly and fast. There might be messages of love and support or the strong urging of someone waiting decades, even generations to speak.

She saw the reactions. She could feel the energy moving and the way the heavy emotions cleared from the room when the evidence was strong. She saw the gratitude and witnessed how people saw me differently after I brought through their loved ones.

On her last day in town, we woke up early and went to the beach to watch the sunrise. Her son had been up late playing video games and would sleep in until almost lunch, so we had plenty of time.

"Can you even remember my life a year ago?" I asked Jae. The sun was just peeking up over the water. We were on towels. I had my legs stretched out in front of me and was leaning back on my hands. Jae had her knees tucked under her chin. She wiggled her toes in the sand.

"I'm so glad you're not still dating Gunther," she said with relief. "Do you ever think about him?"

"I do," I looked out over the water. "Natalie was right. I just needed to give myself everything I was trying to get from him."

"That makes sense." She took a scoopful of sand and poured it over her toes.

"I still love him," I admitted.

Jae gave me the side eye.

"Hear me out," I said, "Part of why it was so hard to get over him was because I thought I'd have to hate him to let him go. I couldn't do it. Then, I realized I didn't have to force myself to stop loving him to let him go. I didn't need to love less. I needed to love more. I needed to include myself."

A large wave crashed on the sand and we both watched it closely to see if we'd have to move back a couple inches as the tide came in.

"Love your neighbor as you love yourself." I quoted. "We're so fixated on the first part we forget about the second part. We are supposed to love ourselves, too. In fact, loving ourselves is the standard. If we don't love ourselves well, we won't love others well, either."

I remembered seeing Gunther from God's eyes on my couch. I had learned that his rejection had nothing to do with me. He wasn't rejecting me, he was rejecting love.

"He didn't know how to love me because he didn't know how to love himself," I said quietly. "And I didn't know how to love him because I didn't love myself either." I took a deep breath then said it. I said what I had learned, "we were the same."

Jae turned her head to look at me and we made eye contact. We were both crying. Her blue eyes were bloodshot and filled with tears.

I tried to wipe my tears away but only smeared my cheeks and eyes with rough sand.

"Why am I like this!?" I screamed out laughing while crying because I couldn't even wipe my tears properly. Jae laughed too, wiping her own tears off elegantly with the back of her wrist.

Another wave crashed and this time, we had to pick up our towels and move farther back on the beach.

"Do you ever hear from James?" Jae asked as we got settled.

"No, I've never even run into him. Maybe he moved away."

We were both quiet. While both of us had never found true love in a man, it somehow felt easier to be in our shoes than in his, finding it and losing it. I didn't quite agree it was better to have loved and lost than to never have loved at all. It seemed like both were unbearably hard.

"It's just the beginning," Jae said. "You can't stop now. I mean, literally, you have an obligation. People are in so much pain and you are helping them. Every time you doubt yourself, you're robbing someone of the opportunity to receive their message and their healing."

Her words hit me with unexpected force. The rising sun cast her profile in gold light.

"Every time you apply for another job only to be told you don't have enough experience, you don't have this or that certification," she continued, "it is an insult to these gifts."

I watched a small wave crash against the shore. She wasn't wrong.

"Have you ever noticed," she said, "that every time you try to *earn* something, like your degree, a promotion, a raise, love from a man then you get knocked down and shut down? But this... It just showed up out of nowhere and continues to give you fulfillment. You are meeting amazing people. Opportunities are just showing up. Every time you give a reading or get on stage, something remarkable happens. You're a new person. Not a different person, but something has profoundly shifted in you ... *you're happy*."

The pattern was unmistakable once she laid it out. All those years of striving, proving, working harder, and here was this gift that had simply arrived, asking only that I trust it. And each time it did, I felt like my life had meaning.

"It's almost as if," she said, her voice softer now, "when you stop trying so hard, the right things will just happen."

"You're right," I said. I was already starting to notice this but her words made it crystal clear. I was struggling because I was trying to squeeze myself into a life that wasn't meant for me. I didn't need to work harder, I needed to slow down so I could listen to the nudges and feel my way into what was showing up for me.

"Just claim it," she stated. "You don't have to earn it. You are it."

Chapter Sixty-One

Matilda

The more readings I gave in more environments, the stronger my connection became. When I treated the challenges as opportunities to learn and refine, my readings got stronger.

Then, instead of seeing a spirit with their pet by their side or on their lap, I started to hear from the pet directly!

At the end of a demonstration for about fifteen people, right before closing my attention was drawn to a woman in the third row, and before I could stop myself, I said, "I think there's a dog in spirit you need to connect with."

"I have a few very loved pets in spirit," she confirmed. "So, it's possible!"

She was open and receptive, so I went for it.

"This dog is small and very low to the ground. I think she's brown. She has a big belly that is distinguishable."

When I leaned over to express this dog physically, I felt my own belly hang down, and the dog gave me an enthusiastic sense of recognition, "Yes, just like that! Ohh, feel that big belly."

"Yes, I think I know who you are talking about," she confirmed.

"She's got floppy ears," I said. "Big floppy ears."

"Yes," her owner confirmed. "I know exactly who that is!"

"Okay," I said, settling into this energy.

Sometimes, it's helpful to build the connection by repeating the evidence out loud. Often, when I do that, new pieces will flow next.

"She's a female dog. She's small and low to the ground. She's a brown color with big floppy ears, and her belly hangs down, almost to the ground." As I was recounting the details again, I leaned over, and my attention was immediately drawn back to my own belly hanging down when I bent over.

"Yes, just like that!" the dog said excitedly. I immediately stood up straight again.

Now, dogs don't judge themselves, and this dog wasn't judging me, but I'm still human, so I judge myself at times. I've been struggling with weight gain from stress and menopause, so I did not like my attention being drawn to my belly, but it was evidence of this dog in spirit, not a condemnation of me, so I shared it.

"Every time I lean over, she gets excited about my belly because it reminds her of her own. She loved her belly," I said. "That's not evidential, because how would you know that, but you would know she was a proud dog, and she had a confident air about her and a decisiveness in her gait."

"Oh yes," her owner confirmed, giggling.

"Her name..." I felt like she was giving me a name. "It starts with an M. I'm not sure of the full name, but she says it's related to a TV show or cartoon, something for kids."

"Matilda. There's a children's book called Matilda. That was her name."

"Thank you," I said. "Matilda, okay. Matilda."

"Matilda is showing me leather shoes. She has a pile of them. They are mismatched and chewed. She would find these shoes and take off with them so she could chew them. You would remember her destroying quite a few of them, mostly, if not all leather boat shoes or loafers."

"Yes."

"And it was a big problem that she destroyed all these shoes. She knew that she was absolutely not supposed to touch them. She knew the rules. And yet she still did it, with glee. She was always looking for an opportunity. Either the consequences were not very harsh or her desire for these shoes was stronger. Nothing could stop her from these shoes."

"Probably both," her owner confirmed. "I was not very good at disciplining her. We tried to keep the shoes away from her, but my husband would forget to put them up, and she'd get them every time."

"She really loved those shoes," I said. "I mean, she would do anything to get a leather shoe in her mouth is what she's making me feel. There is no consequence that would dissuade her. Those shoes, the leather, how her saliva would bring out the juice in the leather. She'd chew on the heel but then shove her nose into the foot and inhale the stinky, musty, sweaty foot odor."

The way Matilda described the scents, textures, and how she became consumed with every part of the shoe felt borderline inappropriate for polite company. I was holding my hands up to my face, describing how Matilda would get her snout into those shoes. It was sexual. It was graphic. Matilda was passionately in love with those leather shoes.

"Good grief, Matilda!" I said out loud. The audience was laughing. It was as if they could read Matilda's mind as well.

"I'm going to try to get some different evidence from Matilda, but I will just say that her passion for those shoes was intense, and Matilda is a very strong communicator!"

Her owner was now wiping a tear of laughter from her eye, and the rest of the audience was chuckling too.

"There was a big production for Matilda's death," I said. "A ceremony was held. Matilda says it wasn't as well attended as a funeral for a president, but it was just as dignified and important. Does that make sense?"

"Yes," My daughters had a ceremony for her in the back yard. It was very significant, and they made it a big event."

"Matilda is very thankful she was given that honor. And she said it was fitting because she was very important."

"Yes, she was very important. We all loved her very much."

"Thank you so much for sharing her with us all."

As I drove home that night, I couldn't stop thinking about Matilda and her strong, unapologetic passion for shoes, her confident demeanor, and the beautiful way she embraced her short, stout body exactly as she was.

Chapter Sixty-Two

Can Mediumship Be Measured?

My hunger to improve the quality of my evidence inspired me to be creative. There had to be a way to improve without hiring a mentor or taking expensive classes. I had always found a way and I knew I'd find something.

I started recording my sessions and studying the evidence I provided along with the validations. I kept a list with the kind of evidence I gave, how specific it was, how often a sitter would validate it. It was tedious work, and very cringey as I watched myself on screen.

Then I realized, I could use Artificial Intelligence to help me collect, organize and rate the evidence, in seconds. I started to train my Large Language Model AI to read the transcripts to pull out each piece of evidence, give it a score, confirm if it was validated and then give me a report card.

This wasn't about proving my abilities or competing. It was about understanding my own patterns, strengths, and growth areas.

I trained it to understand my goals and values. I trained it rate the evidence. And then I would load the transcripts of my readings with a detailed prompt that asked for specific feedback.

Session Analysis Summary:

32 distinct pieces of evidence

85% validated by the sitter

Average specificity score: 7.7/10

I discovered patterns in my readings I never would have noticed otherwise. For instance, my connections were strongest when I started with sensory impressions before moving to visual ones. That single insight transformed how I approached each reading. I studied the trends refined my technique and evaluated my growth.

AI gave me details, data, and trends in seconds. It was a personal coach giving me data and a bird's-eye view of my mediumship practice that I never had before for FREE.

AI can't measure the healing that takes place in a reading, but it helped me identify what could be measured and improved and gave me a way to see my quality and watch it improve.

Chapter Sixty-Three

Manifestation Fulfilled

J ust before Christmas, my friend Kristin who had been a source of constant support and encouragement, even helping me set up chairs, check off names and keep a running list of evidence at my events texted me in the middle of the morning. She sent a long wall of text that sounded frantic. She and I had both been struggling financially and shared our frustrations and fears with each other by sending each other screen shots of our bank balances when they were in the 2 digits. Somehow, both of us were still surviving with more than enough to get by but not much else. Having someone to laugh at the struggle made it feel less isolating. At least we had those two digits, and a paycheck on the way. It was just a matter of making it to payday.

She'd applied for a debt reconsolidation program to turn her situation around. My plan was to rent out my house and go live with my parents for a couple years to get back on track. I joked to her that I'd rent a spare room in her house to stay in when I was in town. I just needed a bed and a desk. While this was an option, I also wanted to keep my house so my kids had somewhere to come home to.

But now, Kristin was facing a new, unexpected financial hurdle.

"My landlord is raising my rent $400 a month! I can't pay that! And I can't go anywhere else now either, my credit is shot!"

Debt reconsolidation was working for her. She was getting her loans paid down but had completely stopped her social life, had stopped getting her hair done, and had become more reclusive because there wasn't money to go out. She had cut back everywhere possible. An extra four hundred a month seemed like a cruel obstacle right when she was turning things around.

Without thinking more than a second, I said, "It will be ok. You can move in with me."

I had a room over my garage with a private bathroom and a large closet that would be plenty for her to have private space. Additionally, my kids would both be in college but could keep their rooms downstairs next to my bedroom. The house had natural separation and enough space for all of us.

The decision was made immediately. It felt right for Kristin. It felt right to me. It helped her financially and even charging her less than half the rent she was paying to live on her own, that would translate to almost a thousand dollars a month income for me to relieve my own financial burden, without having to leave my home or sacrifice my kid's space.

And then it hit me. Not only did I have more than enough for my own security in my house, but I had enough to provide security and be a support to someone I cared about. My manifestation was being fulfilled. It didn't look how I imagined it would need to look when I visualized tens of thousands of dollars in my bank. And it didn't happen overnight. I was still cash strapped. But it showed me I didn't need to have a lot to have more than enough.

I didn't need money to be wealthy. I'd just manifested financial gain with ease, because I had more than enough for my own security and could be her safety net with ease and friendship in a way that benefitted us both! In fact, the way it happened was so subtle, I easily could have missed that this too, was a prayer fulfilled. How many other prayers are answered every day that I miss because I'm expecting it to look different?

I started to look at my life differently and noticed more and more synchronicities. Meeting the exact person, hearing the exact words I needed to nudge me along. I felt more relaxed and trusting. Instead of waiting for the next shoe to fall, I started to keep an eye out for the next miracle.

Jae and I started a list of phrases we told ourselves like mantras to get our mind out of a rut and one of them was "It has nothing to do with me." I repeated this to myself when I was rejected for every job I applied for. I said it when I planned an event and only two people showed up. But I also repeated it when I planned an event and 40 people showed up, when the evidence brought "wow's." Because none of it had anything to do with me. It was because I was aligning with my path. I was following the nudges. If it is meant for me, there is nothing I can do to block it, and if it is not meant for me, there's nothing I can do to earn it.

When things started to feel hard, unpleasant or unfulfilling, I no longer took that as a sign I needed to fix myself or work harder. Instead, I saw that as a nudge to move in a different direction or even, (this one was huge for me) do nothing.

I was healing my heart, my faith and my nervous system. I was slowing down and letting the nudges show me where to go. When I slowed down, I started to imagine a different future for myself as a published author, a speaker. I imagined time for family and friends, travel to new places. I started to say to myself, "It feels so good to be a published author! It feels so good to finally finish my first book!"

I wasn't just imagining my future, I started to create new possibilities for it. You. Yes you! You, reading these words right now. I imagined you. I imagined this moment into reality. Thank you for being a part of my life.

Chapter Sixty-Four

Odie

More and more pets started to come through at demonstrations, and then in my private appointments, too.

A friend from work booked an appointment. She'd been to the demonstration where Matilda shared her love of shoes and wanted to hear from her dog, Odie.

I settled into the connection. Immediately, a black and white dog flashed before my eyes. Lately, my first impression is always a black and white animal. It's never right, but I've learned to trust the process.

Then, I released awareness of myself, allowing Odie to present himself. Suddenly, I felt as though I had a short, pointy brown snout. I was small, but immensely proud. I wasn't just seeing Odie, I was being him.

In mediumship, some spirits stand before me, and I describe them. Others become part of me, and I describe myself as their holographic overlay. Odie became me. I could see his pointy brown nose protruding from my face.

"That sounds like Odie," she said happily.

I continued. "There's something going on with my teeth. One here, one there. Not straight. Missing."

"Yes," She smiled at the evidence. "He lost them all eventually."

I asked him for more evidence. He showed me his bed—round, and perfect for curling up in. Then he shared his joy: bolting out the door. He was very low to the ground, but he knew when the door was even slightly open, and he would rocket out.

"Oh yes!" she confirmed. "He would just take off!"

He also said he loved when she tossed bits of food to him while she was cooking.

"You're a great cook!" I told her.

"I love to cook," she confirmed.

Then, Odie took a different tone. It was confidential, almost conspiratorial. He stood beside me now and whispered in my ear.

"There's something wrong with her," he said.

I didn't know what to do. I knew her from work. We were friends but I didn't know how she would react if I shared that her dog thought there was something wrong with her. And what exactly was wrong?

I'd never had a spirit tell me something I didn't feel comfortable sharing. They were all so loving and comforting. They came forward to apologize or celebrate, never to dish.

"I tried to help. But she won't leave that square," went on.

A square? I must be too far in my head. The messages weren't meant for me, they don't need to make sense to me. Just give what you get, I reminded myself.

"She spends hours every day looking at a square. She won't leave it alone."

She was patiently waiting for me to say more.

A square? I asked Odie. Odie hung his head solemnly. "All day long! There's a window next to her, too, but she doesn't look out the window—she just looks at a square that doesn't even move!"

How was I supposed to convey this? And should I? I didn't want to embarrass her, but I had to trust the message.

"Odie says you spend all day looking at a square," I finally said flatly. Maybe it would make sense to her. It's not for me to decide. I'm just the messenger.

She looked as confused as I felt. But Odie was insistent.

Then, he gave me a flash of her sitting at a desk with a computer screen in front of her.

"See what I mean?" Odie said. He was pacing. "I tried everything to get her to leave that square alone, but she didn't listen to me."

"It's your computer," I clarified. "He's saying you sit at a computer all day and that he used to try to get you to take a break, but you never listened."

"Oh! Yes," she said, suddenly understanding. "Odie would try to get my attention, but I'd be in the middle of something or on a call. He'd give up and just go pee in the house."

I tried to match Odie's serious tone, but I couldn't keep myself from laughing. Soon, I was crying from laughing so hard. I couldn't stop. I had a box of tissue on the table, and this was the first time I needed them for myself. Tears were flowing down my cheeks. I was afraid I was going to pee. I thought of my own dog Domino who must think I'm crazy looking at my square, too!

We sit all day looking at something flat and motionless. No birds or cats racing by. No wind rustling the leaves. No fresh air, nothing to sniff. As far as our pets can tell, we are just staring at screens all day long and it seems crazy! Odies's concern was so touching.

Chapter Sixty-Five

The Mystics in Our Midst

I kept showing up. During my demonstrations, I trusted the process more and more. The more I invested, the more I believed in myself. The more I worked to refine my abilities, the stronger my evidence got. My delivery was improving, and more and more people were showing up to events and booking readings.

The contrast with my job and relationships was undeniable. My energy was being matched, even outdone.

Kristin helped to set up and greet the attendees so I could create mental and spiritual space to center myself before the event. I was learning how to honor myself by sharing the load. People wanted to support me. It wasn't a burden to ask for help.

The events took on a new energy. We were having fun. Instead of worrying what could go wrong, I was excited to see what would go right, who would come through, what they would say. I was excited to meet the people coming to the events as well. A community was forming. After the event, I'd notice people chatting, exchanging numbers, making friendships.

Attending a mediumship demonstration is special. There is an undeniable charge to the energy that feels personal, connecting and magical. After sharing the experience, we feel closer to our loved ones in spirit and each other. Awakening is contagious. We activate and amplify each other, not just at events but everwhere we go.

Most people in the audience had their own stories they wanted to share. They'd had dreams and knowing's. They couldn't explain it, but it was getting harder to ignore and deny. They wanted to meet people who would understand. They wanted to talk about it. They wanted to step into it, with confidence and community. They were mediums and Reiki masters, but also real estate agents, teachers, accountants, and lawyers. They were sound healers, artists, innovators. Their kids were telepathic. The list went on. They were challenging old structures and creating new ones. They were the mystics in our midst, everywhere, curious, awakening and changing the world.

Chapter Sixty-Six

The Evidence is Authenticity

N ow that I've given more readings than I can keep track of and spoken to spirits from more walks of life than I'd ever met before, I've learned something profound: once we're gone, if we're lucky, we might get one last chance to say something to those we leave behind. And if we want it to land with impact and resonance, we need to give the medium evidence of who we truly were, what we cared about, how we made others feel, and what memories we created.

For our loved ones to recognize us through a medium's evidence, we must be seen and known in this life first. Who are you to the people who know you? Are you authentic? No hiding, no minimizing, no shielding? Come as you are! We need to make memories, have passions, step out from behind our screens.

Who I had been for twenty years was not how I wanted to be remembered. I didn't want my kids to think of me as that overextended working mom who cried through lunch, never had time or money for memories, and believed she was replaceable—or worse, disposable.

I needed to change my life to change my story, not only for them but for me too. I needed to start living and embodying the life I was meant for, that we're all meant for.

Already, I'd made many changes: believing in myself, taking chances, walking with faith and courage. But I still needed more memories, more present moments.

It was time to do the things I missed while I was working to be someone I wasn't even meant to be, didn't even want to be. I would live with more heart and less hustle. Everything was going to be fine. I knew it. I believed it. I didn't need to know how. It had nothing to do with me. It was none of my business "how." I needed to believe that everything that is meant for me is ready for me.

I can do this. I can believe anything. I can believe this so intentionally that believing anything else will seem crazy.

I like to imagine what the evidence will be if my kids go to a medium after I die. I'll want to come through a platform medium. I would pick someone brave and uncensored. I'd want to make a scene. I'd have the medium say: "There's a wild old lady here with a hundred chickens all around her. She has the biggest smile and is so full of love. She's got red hair and big boobs. Wow, she's got a sense of humor! She's calling them her melons. She's a free spirit, she just says whatever she wants! And a great communicator! Whew, I can't say that! Wow, she's a great communicator but she's going to get me in trouble! She's telling you to fold the laundry. This is random but I've got to say it. Fold the laundry. Fold the laundry and spend the money! No, don't spend it, just give it away. Maybe both. Just don't keep it. There's way too much money!"

I'd want to give them the same wish my cousin Jae wished for me in her manifestation journal:

"To find peace in her heart and soul to be your own source of fulfillment. To love and accept yourself unconditionally. To embrace 'anything is possible.' Dream Big."

I'd imagine my kids' hearts expanding into colored light connecting them to everyone and everything: to the medium, to the participants, the staff and to all the spirits hovering near their loved ones hoping to say something. The web of lights would flicker and glow in a rainbow of colors, textures and intensities, each completely unique and stunningly beautiful.

About the author

Kathryn Brewer is an evidential medium, mystic, Akashic reader, writer and coach with a gift for translating the unseen into the unforgettable. She left her corporate career in June 2025, shortly after publishing this book, to work full-time in spiritual service. She now helps people connect with thir loved ones in spirit, access soul-level clarity through the Akashic Records, and strengthen their own intuition through classes and coaching.

Today, she gives readings, leads demonstrations, coaches clients speaks at events and writes about the messy, honest reality of spiritual awakening. She lives in North Carolina and believes that sensitivity isn't a flaw, it's a super power.

Not Your Mother's Mystic is her first book.

Connect with Kathryn at https://www.GoldenAgeMedium.com or on Instagram @GoldenAgeMedium

You can find more of Kathryn's writing on Substack where she shares deleted chapters from "Not Your Mother's Mystic," excerpts from her next book and insights on life as a working mystic. To find her substack, go to https://theintuitionage.substack.com or link to it from the Blog tab on GoldenAgeMedium.com

To bring Kathryn to your event or to book a one-on-one reading, vist her website www.GoldenAgeMedium.com

Epilogue

I published "Not Your Mother's Mystic" three weeks after having surgery to remove both ovaries. (I'm fine! It all went well.) I had been rushing to put the final touches on the book in the hopes that book sales would help bridge the gap between disability insurance and my bills while I was recovering. I'd been feeling extremely burnt out at work, overwhelmed from school and needed a break more than anything. I didn't think that break would come in the form of a health concern. That was some sloppy manifesting if you ask me!

But it all works out just as it's meant to. During my recovery, I decided there was no way I could go back to my job. If I was going to do this, I was going to over do it. Waiting for a savings, a safety net, proof or a guarantee would mean I would have to wait for ever. There was no perfect time. The time was now. So, I resigned from my job and dove into this wild, wonderful world of spirit like an enormous trust fall into the unknown.

And God caught me. You caught me. My community, friends and family caught me.

I have no idea what's coming next but I know it's going to be wonderfully surprising and better than I can imagine.

Here is Jae's manifestation journal. Dream Big.

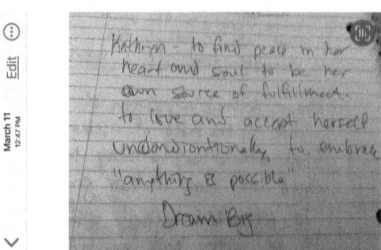

*Jae's Entry in her manifestation
journal*

Testimonials

Kathryn provided SO much verifiable evidence that there was no doubt that she was communicating with my son. I love how she brought herself into the reading, I loved her setup and the clear instructions, including what to expect, and how she works. I loved how she showed how our son's personality was showing up for her. It made it personal, meaningful, and fun. She was 99% accurate in the evidence she brought forward. I am so grateful to her for her work.

Kathryn is a miracle. Her gifts are divinely appointed. She knew nothing about me and yet she easily connected with my mom immediately. I only answered yes or no, so there was no way for her to bring forward the information she did unless she was truly connecting with my mom. She shared things that only my mom would know and captured her essence instantly. I was overwhelmed with joy and sadness, all blended together for absolute gratitude. I received my mom's messages loud and clear and feel an intense sense of inner peace and calm just one hour after our session.

Kathryn was fantastic! She immediately had contact with the person we were seeking, described him, and even said, verbatim, something he had had said to me. The session gave me comfort and is helping me to accept the things that I have experienced as messages from my loved one. Thank you, Kathryn!

It took me a little while to process the session I had withKathryn because it was so incredible. I know without a doubt that she connected to my dad. It was an incredibly powerful and meaningful session that touched me deeply.

I felt very comfortable immediately with you. It was impressive how self-confident and doubtless you were.

I love attending your demonstrations! Even when I don't have a message come through for me personally, I find the evening so uplifting and inspirational. The energy is so positive, and it always intrigues me what messages everyone's loved ones want to bring through. It is always so mind-blowing, the accuracy, kindness, and compassion with which Kathryn receives and communicates each message. What a gift you are; keep up the good work!!!

I am so happy that I attended your wonderful mediumship demonstration! I still find it mind-boggling that my most cherished ones are with me! I have been teary in a great way. Thank you for everything. You put me at ease and bolstered my belief in the hereafter. My heart is full of emotion and my spirit is forever changed."

Early Book Reviews

"You're not just a writer; you're a ghost writer!" Dad

   "I knew you could do it!" Mom

   "Yippee! You did it!" Daughter

   "This isn't even real." Son

   "What's your next book going to be about?" Jae

Resources for Healing

If this book stirred something within you—questions, grief, or a yearning for deeper connection—know that you're not alone. The following organizations have been instrumental in my journey, offering support, insight, and community. I share them here in the hope they may serve you as well.

VerySoul www.verysoul.com

A woman-owned public benefit company connecting individuals with skilled,verified mediums worldwide. VerySoul offers online sessions focused on evidence, healing, and accessibility including free services for those in need.

Suzanne Giesemann www.SuzanneGiesemann.com

A former U.S. Navy Commander turned evidential medium and spiritual teacher. Suzanne offers courses, meditations, and daily messages through her AwakenedWay™ teachings, guiding individuals to connect with higher consciousness and discover their soul's purpose.

Jade's Wings www.JadesWings.com

Intuitive grief counseling and healing services that blend professional support with spiritual insight, helping individuals navigate deep loss with compassion and clarity.

Helping Parents Heal www.HelpingParentsHeal.com

A nonprofit organization supporting bereaved parents by encouraging open conversations about spiritual experiences and afterlife evidence in a safe, uplifting community.

988 Suicide &Crisis Lifeline 988lifeline.org

If you or someone you love is struggling with suicidal thoughts or emotional distress, help is available 24/7. Call or text 988 to speak with trained crisis counselors who are ready to listen and support you.

Please note: These organizations are listed as helpful resources. Their inclusion does not imply endorsement of this book or its contents.

www.ingramcontent.com/pod-product-compliance
Lightning Source LLC
Chambersburg PA
CBHW031503120626
46545CB00005B/1728